ARMS CONTROL AND EAST-WEST RELATIONS

Arms Control
and East-West Relations

Philip Towle

CROOM HELM
London & Canberra

ST. MARTIN'S PRESS
New York

© 1983 Philip Towle
Croom Helm Ltd, Provident House, Burrell Row,
Beckenham, Kent BR3 1AT

British Library Cataloguing in Publication Data

Towle, Philip
    Arms control and East-West relations.
    1. Arms control. 2. Soviet union –
    Foreign relations – 1975
    I. Title
    327.1'74   JX1974
    ISBN 0-7099-2416-X

Library of Congress Cataloging in Publication Data

Towle, Philip, 1945 -
    Arms control and East-West relations.
    Includes index.
    1. Arms control. 2. International relations.
    I. Title.
JX1974.T65   1983   327.1'74   83-2905
ISBN 0-312-04945-5

Printed and bound in Great Britain by
Biddles Ltd, Guildford and King's Lynn

CONTENTS

To Veronica

ABBREVIATIONS

ABM	Anti-ballistic missile
BW	Biological weapons
CBM	Confidence building measure
CCD	Conference of the Committee on Disarmament
CD	Disarmament Committee
CSCE	Conference on Security and Co-operation in Europe
CTBT	Comprehensive Test Ban Treaty
CW	Chemical Weapons
GCD	General and complete disarmament
IAEA	International Atomic Energy Agency
ICBM	Intercontinental ballistic missile
IISS	International Institute for Strategic Studies
IRBM	Intermediate-range ballistic missile
MBFR	Mutual and Balanced Force Reductions
MDW	Mass destruction weapons
MIRV	Multiple independently-targeted re-entry vehicle
MRBM	Medium-range ballistic missile
NATO	North Atlantic Treaty Organisation
NPT	Nuclear Non Proliferation Treaty
NWFZ	Nuclear weapon free zone
NWS	Nuclear weapon state
SALT	Strategic Arms Limitation Treaty
SIPRI	Stockholm International Peace Research Institute

INTRODUCTION

Arms control is unpopular today. On the one side it is attacked by those who hope to achieve the abolition of armaments or General and Complete Disarmament (GCD) because they feel that arms control measures have failed to curb the arms race. On the other side it is criticised by those who believe that the arms control agreements of the 1960s and 1970s enabled the Soviet Union to forge ahead of the West in the accumulation of armaments.

This situation is in sharp contrast with the one prevailing between 1963 and 1977. At that time GCD was discredited. The interminable disarmament negotiations between East and West in the 1950s had produced not a single agreement. As Evan Luard put it in a book first published in 1968,

> long hours of negotiation and countless flights of ingenuity were diverted to attempts to devise a foolproof system for control over the manufacture and possession of nuclear weapons. Yet, either publicly or privately, virtually all powers admitted foolproof control to be unattainable.[1]

In contrast the 1960s and 1970s saw the negotiation of a series of limited arms control measures, that is to say agreements designed to 'stabilise' the East-West military balance and to reduce the unpredictability of international relations rather than necessarily to lower force levels. These began with the Partial Test Ban Treaty of 1963 and continued until the signature of the Environmental Modification Treaty in 1977. Governments and commentators hoped that this process would improve East-West relations and gradually lead to more far-reaching measures. But this second hope has not so far been fulfilled. It proved more and more difficult to find worthwhile arms control measures which did not require on-site inspection to ensure that they were being observed. Yet such inspection was one of the prime stumbling blocks to the disarmament negotiations in the 1950s.

More importantly the atmosphere of detente, which the partial arms control measures had helped to foster, began to deteriorate. Primarily this was because of the profound political differences between the communist and democratic worlds which arms control alone could

1

not bridge. These differences were reflected in US-Soviet disagreements over Soviet activities in Africa, Afghanistan and elsewhere. The decline of detente was accentuated by the belief that the Russians had taken advantage of detente to strengthen their relative military position. Suspicion also began to grow that the USSR was not abiding by some of the arms control agreements which had been negotiated and thus the agreements themselves contributed to the polarisation of Western opinion. As detente declined, so the fear of war grew amongst the general public and disarmament again became a rallying cry in opposition to arms control. It is against this background that this book has been written in the hope that, in future, we may have a more realistic idea of the place which arms control can occupy in East-West relations.

The efficacy of arms control was undoubtedly exaggerated during the 1960s and 1970s. Arms control is to international relations in general and to warfare in particular as aspirin is to the diseases found in man. If the disease is really serious then aspirin is ineffective; if political relations between states are sufficiently bad, then arms control agreements are unattainable. Conversely, if relations improve beyond a certain point, then arms control negotiations are unnecessary. It is only in the intermediate band of relationships that arms control or 'stabilising' measures are worthwhile and effective. The difficulty in the crucial cases is to determine the seriousness of the disease. Until the Munich agreement of 1938 the British Prime Minister, Neville Chamberlain, continued to discuss limitations on bomber aircraft with the Nazi government. In retrospect this effort appears naive or foolhardy and it may have contributed to Hitler's belief that the democracies would try to avoid war at almost any cost. It certainly reflected Chamberlain's inability to assess the seriousness of the 'illness'. Hitler was determined to overthrow the European *status quo* and, if his revisionist aims were not accepted, then they had to be opposed by force rather than by treaty.

If arms control corresponds to aspirin, the level of armaments corresponds to the patient's temperature. Thus, if the international situation deteriorates, so the level of armaments will rise, not in the short term but as quickly as governments can mobilise their resources. Just as in really serious illnesses aspirin will fail to keep down the patient's temperature so, when international relations deteriorate beyond a certain point, arms control treaties will be denounced or ignored. Arms control is not a panacea therefore. Just as aspirin can, alongside other medicines, make a significant contribution to making illness more bearable in less serious cases, so arms control can reduce the 'pain' involved in East-West relations. This book is based on the belief that, primarily because of nuclear deterrence, our relationship with the Soviet Union is not 'terminal' and that arms control has a part to play, alongside defence and deterrence, in stabilising East-West relations and reducing the likelihood of war.

The crux of the argument in the first or strategic section of this book is that wars are not caused by armaments, anymore than a patient's illness is caused by the rise in his temperature — though that rise can sometimes have unfortunate effects. Illness is caused by bacteria and wars are caused by politics, by the desire of revisionist states, such as Hitler's Germany, to change the *status quo*. However these desires will only lead to war if the military omens are favourable. In the past the pressure for disarmament has sometimes actually increased the likelihood of war because it operates most effectively in a *status quo* power and, by reducing the strength of such states, it has given the revisionists the opportunity to attack. Similarly those in favour of more limited arms control measures have sometimes had the same effect. By striving to equalise the power of potential enemies, they have occasionally increased the relative strength of the revisionists. Fortunately in the nuclear age what matters to a large extent for the Great Powers is the security of their nuclear retaliatory forces not the military balance. Arms control agreements can thus be designed to equalise the nuclear forces of such powers without making war more likely. However, the main danger of a confrontation between the Soviet Union and the USA comes from their involvement in conflicts in the Third World and I have suggested ways in which their direct involvement might be reduced.

The most fundamental way of tackling the problem is nevertheless to go to the political kernel of the dispute between East and West and to try to reduce political tensions. Some would, of course, argue that the idea is absurd, firstly because rivalry between Great Powers is 'natural' and inevitable. But the degree of rivalry, the ferocity of the competition is not a constant. Britain and the USA were 'natural' rivals in the twentieth century because they were both world trading powers with major surface fleets. However, they never fought, despite occasional friction. Conversely, British and German strategic and economic interests were complementary. Before the First World War much of their trade was with each other, yet they fought for ten years. Rivalry leading to war cannot therefore be assumed, although really intense political divisions cannot be bridged by negotiations. No doubt, hostility between the Protestant and Catholic kingdoms in seventeenth-century Europe would have been lessened had either abandoned the tenets of their faith or been prepared to tolerate alternative beliefs. But that was precisely what they were not prepared to do.

The negotiators at the Conference on Security and Co-operation in Europe, which met from 1973 to 1975, were thus aware that the ideological division of Europe could not be removed and that they would have to be satisfied with more limited aims. The East wanted some recognition of the frontiers imposed by the Soviet Union on the area in 1945. The West wanted to see some freedom of information and movement across the Iron Curtain. The result of the conference was to encourage the 'human rights' movement in Poland and elsewhere in the East, thus accentuating the political weakness of the Soviet bloc. At the same time it led to a more rapid reduction in Western than in Soviet military preparations. This in turn could create a dangerous situation if the Soviet leaders were encouraged to embark on foreign adventures in order to keep their empire together. The 'political' approach thus leads back to arms control and points to the need to co-ordinate CSCE and arms control policies.

In the second or diplomatic section of the book I have looked at the way in which the Soviet Union, the Third World and the West regard arms control and disarmament, and the possibilities which their attitudes raise for constructive agreements. The Russians take a much more consistent and strategic approach towards arms control than the democracies. They are not swayed by the forces of public opinion and they can look after their strategic interests much more single-mindedly than Western states can. On the other hand, the development of nuclear weapons has given them an interest in arms control which the dictators of the 1930s certainly did not have. The Third World states advocate the disarmament of the Great Powers but rarely consider arms control in their own regions. They act as the chorus to the central negotiations. For the democracies, on the other hand, arms control is a natural part of their defence and foreign policies. A fact exemplified at the time of writing by the decision of the Reagan administration in the USA to begin negotiations with the Soviet Union, despite the previous hostility of members of the administration to such initiatives.

Because the essence of the problem is political, the most difficult and vital part of arms control is verification. If there were no fears and suspicions, there would be no arms and no reasons for arms control. Because the fears and suspicions remain, agreements have to be effectively verified. However, close examination of the problem of inspection in the interwar period did little but expose the difficulties involved. In the 1950s the invention of nuclear weapons enhanced the importance of effective verification but in the following decades the partial arms control measures appeared to have side-stepped the issue by relying upon satellites and other non-intrusive methods of verification. However, the decline of detente in the 1970s showed that such partial verification could mean that agreements actually exacerbated tensions. Thus, the problems analysed in the 1930s revived once again. In the end there can be no escape from the dilemma and arms control can only be effective in stabilising East-West relations to the extent that it can be adequately verified.

Because arms control is so much a natural part of our diplomacy in the West, we must wrestle with these problems. We must also try to organise the negotiations in ways which are most likely to produce constructive results. In the final chapter I look at what these ways might be. If the international 'disease' with which we are faced is not necessarily terminal, and I believe that it is not, then 'aspirin' can make a substantial contribution, alongside other factors, in reducing the pains and tensions involved. Once East-West relations start to improve again what will be needed is a general politico-military settlement stabilising relations and going some way towards preventing the swings between detente and cold war which have characterised the post-1945 period.

Note

1. E. Luard, *Conflict and Peace in the Modern International System*, University of London, 1970, p. 216.

Part One

STRATEGIES

1 THE DISARMER'S APPROACH

For the straightforward disarmers, armaments *per se* are the prime cause of wars and tensions. They would argue that any increase in armaments makes war more likely and conversely that almost any disarmament measure enhances the prospects for peace. Such analysts would therefore believe that there is a necessary contradiction between avoiding war and preparing for it militarily. Each time that the international atmosphere has darkened, before 1914, in the 1930s and again in the 1950s, popular movements have arisen in Britain and in other democracies blaming the arms races for this deterioration.

This point of view, and the belief that the arms race is out of the control of the politicians, again became prevalent in the early 1980s. The Labour Member of the British Parliament, Frank Allaun, wrote to *The Times*: 'at present there is a nuclear arms race, the most terrible the world has ever seen, which can result only as all previous arms races have done,' that is in war.[1] Similarly the former Director of the Stockholm International Peace Research Institute, Frank Barnaby, has argued that the arms race means 'we are drifting inexorably towards nuclear war',[2] whilst Professor Adam Curle, the former Professor of Peace Studies at Bradford University, contends that 'every development in the number and quality of nuclear weapons, whoever holds them, increases the danger of war'.[3] Those who take this point of view then believe that it is the arms race which is responsible for political tensions and not the other way round. Armaments and arms races develop a momentum towards war that escapes from the control of politicians and statesmen.

History

This conception is a relatively modern one. In the nineteenth century there were few who believed that the Crimean War, the American Civil War or the Franco-Prussian War were the results of arms races. In the first two cases at least, all the combatants were clearly unprepared. Thus, many pacifist groups called for the arbitration of international disputes rather than for disarmament as a way of avoiding war. Moreover, their appeals had some effect on policy-makers. At the beginning

9

of the twentieth century President Taft of the United States became an enthusiastic advocate of an arbitration treaty with Britain. Similarly the British Prime Minister, Herbert Asquith, argued,

> what a few years ago might have been regarded as the dream of idealists has not only passed into the domain of practical statesmanship, but has become the settled purpose of two great democracies.[4]

Accordingly on 3 August 1911 the Anglo-American Arbitration Treaty was signed and many other agreements of the same type were negotiated during the period before the First World War. One of the few concrete achievements of the First Hague Peace Conference in 1899 was to establish an international court at The Hague to arbitrate on disputes. The millionaire philanthropist, Andrew Carnegie, agreed to pay for the building to house the court and, when the Palace of Peace opened in 1913, one journalist described it as 'an event of high European importance . . . of vast interest to all civilized nations'. He went on to eulogize its 'monumental tower [which] like a beacon points to the nations' the road of right and justice and truth'.[5] Unfortunately the nations failed to follow this road and in August 1914 the First World War began, following the murder of the Austrian Archduke, Franz Ferdinand. The British Foreign Secretary, Sir Edward Grey, did propose that the dispute should be settled by discussion between representatives of the various states but his proposal simply infuriated the German Kaiser. On a despatch from his ambassador in London he wrote, 'instead of mediation, a serious word to St Petersburg and Paris that England would not help them would quieten the situation at once'.[6] The services of the international court went unused.

After the end of the war further efforts were made to encourage states to resolve their disputes by arbitration and conciliation. In December 1920 the Permanent Court of International Justice was established at The Hague and the new League of Nations fostered various methods of encouraging states to observe a 'cooling off' period before wars began. Yet the heart seems to have gone out of the arbitration movement, at least on the popular level. The anti-war essays of the time, such as Goldsworthy Lowes Dickinson's *War: Its Nature, Cause and Cure*, published in 1923, dismissed arbitration as ineffective because it would never be accepted on major issues. Writing of Sir Edward Grey's proposals for mediation in 1914, Dickinson asked, suppose that sometime in 1920 the Prince of Wales had been murdered by Sinn Feiners in Ireland . . . how should we have felt about the case? How should we have dealt with proposals to submit the dispute to the Hague Court? Can you imagine the fury of the British press?

When he had disposed of arbitration, Dickinson went on to discuss the armed forces and the part which they played in the causes of war. In his view, which became the conventional wisdom of the time,

soldiers . . . imply armaments and think in terms of armaments. It is they who push for the continual growth of armies and navies, of aeroplanes, of poison gas, of all the mechanism of destruction. And, as we have seen, that very growth becomes itself a principal cause of war.[7]

In earlier periods the dictum 'if you wish for peace, prepare for war' had been widely accepted and only ignored when no immediate threat was apparent. But from 1918 to 1934, in Britain at least, the opposite point of view was held by many policy-makers as well as by the public at large. In this respect Sir John Simon, the British Foreign Secretary, told the League of Nations Disarmament Conference in February 1932,

an immense change has come over the judgement of the world. The proposition that the peace of the world is to be secured by preparing for war is no longer believed by anybody, for recent history manifestly disproves it. A high level of armaments is no substitute for security. At best, it only creates the illusion of security in one quarter while at the same time aggravating the sense of insecurity in another.[8]

Simon's claim that no one believed that armaments provided security was an admonition rather than an expression of the facts; as he well knew, the French government very firmly believed that its army provided it with security and France's allies in Eastern Europe endorsed this view equally strongly. Nevertheless, Simon expressed the ideas of the majority of his countrymen who found it difficult to understand French 'intransigence' over disarmament. They believed that every reduction in French armaments would make peace so much more secure because they accepted the view that the First World War had been caused by the arms race.

We can see a number of occasions where this attitude shaped policy. When the Anglo-Japanese alliance ended at the Washington Naval Conference in 1922, the Conservative government in power in Britain decided to build a naval base at Singapore to protect British possessions in Asia and the Pacific from a Japanese attack. However, when the British Labour Party took office, it cancelled the base. Instead it announced in March 1924,

> we stand for a policy of international co-operation through a strengthened and enlarged League of Nations, the settlement of disputes by conciliation and judicial arbitration and the creation of conditions which will make a comprehensive limitation of armaments possible.[9]

Labour leaders felt that if the base went ahead 'it would hamper the establishment of this confidence . . . we should almost inevitably drift into a condition of mistrust and competition of armaments in the Far East'. On their return to power the Conservatives recommenced the base, albeit slowly, and it was not until the Japanese invaded Manchuria in 1931 that the building programme was speeded up.

In retrospect we can clearly see the flaws in both Labour and Conservative party strategy. The Singapore base was never a major irritant in Anglo-Japanese relations. The key to these relations in the 1930s was Japan's desire to dominate Manchuria and other parts of China.[10] If Britain and the other European countries attempted to block Japanese plans for expansion on the Asian continent then relations were bound to deteriorate. The cancellation of the Singapore base had to be accompanied by appeasement of Japanese political ambitions if it were to avoid war. The combination of strategic weakness and political opposition would inevitably prove fatal. Conservative strategy was no more successful because, when the base was complete, it was inadequately defended.

Neither in the Far East nor in Europe were weapons or military preparation in general the prime cause of conflict in the 1930s. After Hitler came to power in Germany, an arms race did gradually develop in Europe but it was caused by Hitler's apparent determination to overthrow the Versailles settlement and to reassert German dominance. Moreover, as many commentators pointed out at the time, the primary arms race often appeared to be between Germany and the Soviet Union. Thus Max Werner argued in a book published by the Left Book Club in 1939, at the head of all other military powers are the two economically strong countries which have at the same time the most highly developed war potential, Germany and the Soviet Union.[11]

Yet, when war came in 1939, it broke out first between Germany and the democracies, just as, before 1914, Britain and Germany which had competed so intensely in naval armaments, were the last to declare war. Nevertheless, armaments were a secondary cause of the outbreak of war in 1939 because Germany overtook, or appeared to overtake, France in terms of military power. Germany was no longer deterred from trying to achieve its political aims, yet Britain and France were not prepared to accept them *in toto*. If the democracies had been prepared to concede German domination without resistance there would have been no war. Again it was the combination of political opposition with strategic weakness, or apparent weakness, which was to prove fatal.

The Postwar World

It is just as difficult to believe that any of the wars since 1945 have been caused primarily by arms races as to believe that these were the main causes of the two world wars. No one seriously contends that the longest and perhaps the most bloody series of wars — in Vietnam — were caused by the armaments in the area. Of course, if the Russians and Chinese had not supplied the communist Vietnamese with armaments, they would have found it more difficult to carry on the struggle against the French and the Americans. Similarly, if the Americans had not supported the French economically and militarily before 1954, they might have pulled out before they were forced to concede defeat at Dien Bien Phu. But the root causes of the wars were political. The determination of the North Vietnamese to control the whole of a communist Vietnam and the determination of the French and American governments to prevent them from doing so.

Similarly in the Middle East, if the Israelis had received no outside support whatsoever, whilst the Arabs had been armed by the Russians, Israel would have been overrun. In this sense the arms available to the Israelis have 'caused' the successive Arab-Israeli wars, or rather have prevented the Arabs achieving a final military solution. But, if neither side had received any assistance from the outside, it is clear that there would still have been wars fought in the Middle East with the combatants using whatever equipment the local inhabitants could fashion for themselves. Indeed, the probability is that the wars would have been more prolonged. Recent wars in the area have come to an end when both sides have run out of advanced equipment. Similarly the casualties caused by more primitive equipment would probably have been greater. On the whole, the more advanced the equipment, the fewer troops would be in the front line and the more the war would come to resemble a battle between rival technologies rather than peoples. It is the primitive guerrilla wars which have caused most casualties amongst the combatants since 1945, not the advanced conventional wars between India and Pakistan, between the Arabs and Israelis or between Britain and Argentina. In any case, the underlying cause of war is the Israeli determination to defend their newly formed state and the determination of the Arabs to restore Israeli lands to the Palestinians.

If any further proof were needed that armaments and arms races are not the prime cause of war, it is that many arms races have petered out without leading to any violence. From time to time in the nineteenth century Britain and France built warships in competition and France was generally regarded by the Royal Navy as its most formidable likely enemy. Thus, in 1889 it was fear of the French navy which led to the passing of the Naval Defence Act providing for a considerable increase in British naval strength. But the competition never led to blows, despite the fact that it was caused by the intense colonial rivalry between the two powers. Similarly Russia and Britain not only competed at sea but were rivals throughout the period in Central Asia. Yet, after 1855, Britain and Russia never fought each other, unless one counts British intervention in the civil war in Russia in 1919, but that occurred precisely when Russian power had collapsed and there was certainly no arms race. In the 1920s the Royal Air Force looked askance at the size of the French forces on the other side of the Channel, whilst the Royal Navy resented the size of the submarine forces deployed by its French neighbours. At the same time, the Royal Navy measured its cruiser strength against the USA and US armed forces prepared plans for a war against Britain.[12] Finally we have the experience of 25 years of military competition between NATO and the Warsaw Pact. Yet not one of these 'arms races' led to war. In some circumstances it seems that military competition can become a substitute for outright conflict.

Some may argue that armaments cause the initial fears and that political disputes emerge afterwards. Britain was not hostile to Germany before 1914 until the Germans began to develop a High Seas Fleet. But it was what that fleet symbolised which seemed threatening to British eyes — the new post-Bismarckian policy of a restless, dissatisfied power, determined to assert itself on the world stage. If armaments alone were enough to cause political fears then all the West European states would today fear the USA which has the power to attack and overrun them. The fact is that arms races cannot be defined *except in political terms*. A spaceman arriving on Earth in 1951 might have been forgiven for believing that an arms race was taking place between the Western nations. Only a knowledge of the political situation would have shown him that Britain and the USA were not arming against each other but against the communist bloc.

Analysts who feed arms race statistics into computers to see if they can be correlated with the outbreak of wars are forced to define the races in terms of political antagonisms, not in terms of armaments. If they did not do so the whole idea would be absurd. Britain and France did not go to war with each other in 1936, nor did Britain and the USA fight in 1951, despite their rearmament. Political hostility is essential if wars are to take place, military preparations are not. They can sometimes be a sign that war is likely but in civil wars such preparations are usually impossible, whilst there have been plenty of occasions, such as the Crimean War or the Argentine intervention in the Falklands in April 1982, when there was virtually no direct military competition beforehand.

Armaments and War

Wars are caused by profound conflicts of political interests, not primarily by armaments or arms races. Why then does the myth that armaments are the main cause of war persist? First of all, those who believe in the myth find armaments emotionally distasteful or frightening because they can kill people. Secondly they frequently want a panacea, something that will prevent wars for all time. Arbitration, as we have seen, has been tried and found wanting. International organisations, such as the League of Nations and the UN, have also been established but they have frequently not succeeded in avoiding war though, like arbitration, they may have reduced its occurrence or duration. Disarmament alone, some might say, has not been attempted. However since arms control and disarmament negotiations have been carried on in peacetime in almost every year since 1918, it would be more accurate to say that it has been attempted but not effectively put into practice.

The third major reason why people blame armaments for war is that armed forces are related in complex ways to the outbreak of conflicts. First of all the timing of war can be determined by the military situation. For example, the Japanese government decided in 1903 that it would go to war with Russia, because the Russian government would not come to a satisfactory agreement on spheres of influence in Manchuria and Korea. Thus, the basic cause of the Russo-Japanese War was political. But the timing of the war was decided by the military situation. The Japanese were determined to strike before the Russian naval build-up in the Far East was complete. However, they also delayed their onslought until the warships being built for them in Europe were safely on their way to Japan.[13] Then they launched a pre-emptive torpedo boat attack on the Russian Pacific Fleet.

Similarly the timing of the Second World War was also partly determined by the state, or the perceived state, of armaments. Britain and France abandoned Czechoslovakia at the Munich Conference in 1938 partly for political reasons, because the British authorities still hoped to come to an agreement with Hitler on a general European settlement. But they also felt too weak militarily to come to Czechoslovakia's defence. A year later they went to war to protect Poland, partly because they had now abandoned hope of appeasing Hitler, and partly because they believed they were in a better position to parry a knock-out blow on London.[14] Furthermore, the military situation determined the timing of the outbreak of war in the Far East which began with the Japanese attacks on Pearl Harbor and Malaya. The Japanese government believed that its economic and military situation would deteriorate, if it postponed its attack beyond December 1941, because the United States had imposed increasingly stringent sanctions on Japan and was in the middle of a massive naval construction programme.[15]

Not only is the timing of war decided very frequently by military considerations but it is often the prospects of victory, or the lack of them, which determine whether a government will make a stand on a particular political issue or give way. Thus, even when a state is threatened with dismemberment — as Czechoslovakia was from 1938 onwards — a government may decide that resistance is still purposeless. Of course, there are some contrary examples where countries have resisted against apparently hopeless odds. Few outside observers would have expected Finland to defend itself successfully against the Soviet Union in December 1939. Yet by resisting, in spite of the low prospects of success, it is arguable that Finland assured its future independence. Despite such examples, it is fair to say that governments and peoples have to believe in the prospects of victory if they are to resist attack. In other words their decision to fight is crucially influenced by their perception of the military balance.

In 1914 the Austrian government decided to use the assassination of the Habsburg heir as an opportunity to crush Serbia, because of the magnet that a strong independent Serbia presented for the Slavs living inside Austrian territory. Vienna's aims were thus profoundly political. The war became general because Russia backed up its fellow Slavs, whilst Germany backed the Austrian government. Miscalculations played an important part, as each side hoped that the other would back down or that the other alliance would not hold together. Armaments and armed forces were influential in two principal ways. First of all the very fact that the two sides to the dispute appeared evenly balanced encouraged each to oppose the political aims of the other. If Russian leaders had believed that they were militarily incapable of going to Serbia's support they would have been forced to back down and to watch Serbia crushed by Austria. If Austria had been weaker and had no German support, it would probably have backed down in the face of Russian protests.

The schedules for mobilising the various armies also contributed to the débâcle in 1914. Prussia had won its victories against Austria-Hungary in 1866 and against France in 1870 partly because of the speed and efficiency with which it mobilised its troops. Hence, by 1914, each of the great continental powers believed that it had to mobilise its land forces rapidly to prevent the other side striking a 'knock-out' blow and each regarded the mobilisation of its potential enemies as a direct threat to its security. All this reduced the time available to statesmen to resolve their political differences. Thus, in August 1914, in September 1939, in December 1941 and on many other occasions when war has broken out since 1945, armaments were not the main cause of the conflict. The primary cause was the political decision of the government taking the initiative to crush its enemies. But strategy influenced such decisions by making victory seem possible. Similarly armaments very often determined the timing of the first battle.

Many of those who believe that armaments are a cause of war, also believe that the arms race is driven by a 'military-industrial' complex and that it is 'out of control'. They conjure up visions of the nations today frantically arming themselves in preparation for war. But the reality is more complex. Much of the equipment in service in Europe and elsewhere is several decades old. The Centurion tank, which was developed in the Second World War, was in service in 1982 with Denmark, Netherlands, Sweden and Switzerland in Europe, as well as with many other nations around the world. The Soviet long-range aircraft — the Badger and Bear — as well as their US equivalent — the B52 — all date from the 1950s.

Modern weapons systems — tanks, ships, warships — take about ten years to develop and remain in service (if successful) for three decades. Thus, research on a weapon might begin in 1961, the weapon might come into service in 1971 and remain in service until 2001. It is this lengthy cycle of research, development and service which convinces so many that the 'arms race' has a life of its own. Evidently the political situation will have changed many times during the 40-year cycle. East-West relations reached their nadir with the first Berlin crisis and the Korean War; they then gradually improved, though with many setbacks, until the second Berlin confrontation and the Cuba crisis; subsequently they began to improve again — a process symbolised by the signature of the Partial Test Ban Treaty in August 1963 and reaching its peak with the signature of SALT 1 in May 1972. There followed a period of slow deterioration with arguments over Cuban intervention in Africa and Soviet intervention in Afghanistan.

The ebb and flow of East-West relations does not and cannot correspond to the life cycle of a weapon. But this does not mean that the ultimate motive for producing such weapons is not political. In periods when no danger threatens a democracy its armaments decline, even if military research establishments are kept in existence. There was a classic example of this in Britain in the 1920s. With no obvious enemy in sight, the research establishments produced designs for improvements in weapons which were promptly shelved. Thus, they worked steadily on a design for a gun which would replace the 18 pounder and the 4.5 inch howitzer. But it was not until 1933 (15 years after the end of the First World War and after Hitler had come to power in Germany) that the War Office decided that a 25 pounder with a calibre of 3.7 inches could replace both the older weapons and it was not until 1934 that a General Staff specification was issued.[16] By 1935 a new 303 calibre rifle had been developed but was shelved through lack of money.[17] Governmental lack of interest was particularly important where tank development was concerned. As this was so expensive few were made and British tanks in the Second World War proved almost uniformly inferior to their German equivalents.[18] The official historians of the British military research establishment summed up the effects of governmental parsimony and indifference in the interwar period briefly and concisely:

> the difficulties involved in nursing enthusiasm in the inter war years
> were very great. How could the head of an establishment encourage
> his technicians to press on with the development of a new device
> when high authority evinced so obvious a lack of interest in reequip-
> ping the armed forces?[19]

It is clear therefore that the 'military-industrial complex' is not
always some state within a state which can force the pace of armaments
development against the wishes of the government. Since 1945 fear of
the Soviet Union in the West has been generally at a level which has encouraged governments to continue plans for replacing equipment as it
became obsolete, though with increasing difficulty as the cost of equipment rose. Personnel levels have been more responsive to political
changes. Thus US forces dropped from over 11.5 million men in 1945
to 1.34 million in 1948. They rose again to 3.5 million as a result of
the Korean War, then gradually declined to 2.5 million in 1960. Subsequently they began to grow slowly, firstly because of the Kennedy
administration's feeling that the nation was relying too much on
nuclear weapons and secondly because of the war in Vietnam. Following the end of that war, conscription was abolished and US forces fell
to two million, though whether they will stay at that level depends
both on the state of relations with the Soviet Union and on the depth
of public hostility towards national service.

Thus changes in strategic doctrine, peripheral wars and the state of
public opinion have all influenced US defence policies and these influ-
ences have not necessarily pushed in the same direction as fears of the
Soviet Union. But to admit that other factors influence the level of the
defence effort, apart from the general international situation, is very
far from asserting that that situation has only a peripheral effect.[20] By
and large the state of a democracy's armaments is determined by the
interaction between the assessment of the threat of war, the need to
economise on military expenditure and the state of military technology. Economics mean that, over a long period of peace, force levels
will generally decline and this is what has happened in the West since
1945. Arms races do not cause war but, even if they did, it is false to
say that we are in the middle of an ever-escalating arms race. The
problem for the West is that we know very little about the processes
which determine the Soviet defence effort. Moreover, as we shall see,
the hope that the progress of detente would lead to a rapid slackening

of this effort, proved to be false (see p. 184).

Proposals

The concern of the disarmament lobby with the 'arms race' may divert attention from more important issues. These are firstly to avoid, as far as possible, developing weapons or defence policies which would in a crisis reduce the time available for statesmen to make 'rational' decisions. As far as strategic nuclear weapons are concerned, this means avoiding weapons which we would have to 'launch on warning' immediately we thought that the Soviets were about to attack. Secondly we have to design our defence effort and our arms control policies so as to reduce the possibility that, if the political conflict intensified, the Kremlin might see hopes of destroying our forces before we had any chance to respond.

Thirdly, the disarmament lobby would be wise to push for agreements in those rare areas where economic pressures are less effective at limiting the manufacture of weapons. It seems likely that the production of fissile material for nuclear weapons is one of these. Once the production facilities are established the cost of producing extra warheads and bombs is relatively low. In the 1960s the USA pushed for a treaty banning the production of fissile material for nuclear weapons. This was opposed by the Soviet Union probably partly because it felt that the USA was far ahead in the accumulation of fissile material at that time. Furthermore, the Americans wanted to verify the observance of the treaty by some form of inspection on all nuclear facilities. Today a 'cut-off' in the production of such fissile material could be verified by applying inspection by the International Atomic Energy Agency (IAEA) to all nuclear facilities in the NWS, just as the IAEA now inspects the nuclear power stations in those countries which have signed the Nuclear Non-Proliferation Treaty. This would seem a very effective way of limiting strategic nuclear weapons and supplementing the Strategic Arms Limitation (SAL) negotiations. It would therefore be worthwhile trying to persuade the Soviet Union to change its stand on verification and it is surprising that the contemporary disarmament lobby does not appear to have appreciated the importance of the issue.

In the West a 'cut-off' would reduce the prevalent and divisive fears of armaments and particularly of nuclear armaments. Whilst in East-West terms it would have great symbolic significance, solidifying a new period of detente. In general it would separate nuclear energy and nuclear weapons and allow the case for nuclear energy to stand or fall upon its own merits. Above all a 'cut-off' would not destabilise the *status quo* and it would be effectively verifiable. Thus, if and when East-West relations once again deteriorated, it would not contribute to mutual suspicions in the way that some unverified arms control measures have done.

Notes

1. *The Times*, 14 March 1981. For a slightly more agnostic view see J.D. Singer (ed.), *The Correlates of War*, The Free Press, New York, 1979, pp. 145-54.
2. Loc cit., 2 August 1981.
3. Loc cit., 9 May 1981.
4. Quoted in W.L. Grane, *The Passing of War*, Macmillan, London, 1912, p. 72.
5. William Caird, 'the World's temple of peace', *British Review*, September 1913.
6. Prince Lichnowsky, *Heading for the Abyss*, Constable, London, 1928, p. 406.
7. G. Lowes Dickinson, *War: Its Nature, Cause and Cure*, Allen and Unwin, London, 1923, pp. 70 and 119.
8. Speech by the Rt Honourable Sir John Simon, MP, reproduced as *Miscellaneous No 3, 1932*, Cmd 4018, p. 4.
9. Cabinet papers, Public Record Office, London, CAB/23/47.
10. Nicholas Clifford, *Retreat from China*, Longmans, London, 1967, p. 147.
11. Max Werner, *The Military Strength of the Powers*, Gollancz, London, 1939, p. 19.
12. G. Jordan (ed.), *Naval Warfare in the Twentieth Century*, Croom Helm, London, 1977, p. 167 passim.
13. Philip Towle, 'British assistance to the Japanese Navy during the Russo-Japanese War of 1904-5', *The Great Circle*, April 1980.
14. For fears of such a blow, see Uria Bialer, *The Shadow of the Bomber*, Royal Historical Society, London, 1980.
15. See note 10 supra. See also J.H. Herzog, *Closing the Open Door*, Naval Institute Press, Annapolis, 1973, and S.E. Pelz, *Race to Pearl Harbor*, Harvard University Press, 1974.
16. M.M. Postan, D. Hay and J.D. Scott, *The Design and Development of Weapons*, HMSO, London, 1964, p. 255 passim.
17. Ibid.
18. G. Macleod Ross, *The Business of Tanks*, Ilfracombe, Devon, 1976.
19. Postan, Hay and Scott, *Design and Development of Weapons*, p. 435.
20. For the opposite point of view, see M. Kaldor, 'the decadence of baroque arms', *Guardian*, 18 January 1982.

2 THE ARMS CONTROL APPROACH

The Fallacy of Equality

Long before the term 'arms control' was widely used, democratic governments spent their time trying to negotiate agreements which would stabilise their military relationships with other states. Normally this meant trying to equalise the military power of the various countries. Even today there is a very general tendency to assume that the primary aim of many of the current arms control negotiations is to equalise the armed forces of East and West. The West hopes that the talks on Mutual and Balanced Force Reduction (MBFR) will bring conventional forces in Central Europe down to an equal level on both sides. The SAL agreements impose equal upper limits on US and Soviet strategic forces. Such treaties appear to be predicated on the assumption that, if US and Soviet, NATO and Warsaw Pact armies and armaments were reduced to the same size this would decrease the likelihood of war. This assumption is evidently linked to the conventional idea that, as President Mitterand of France put it in his first press conference after his election, 'only the balance of forces preserves peace'.[1] Yet this idea is false. As Geoffrey Blainey has argued in his analysis of the *Causes of War*,

> the idea that an even distribution of power promotes peace has gained strength partly because it has never been accompanied by tangible evidence . . . the military power of rival European alliances was most imbalanced, was distributed most unevenly, at the end of a decisive war. And decisive wars tended to lead to long periods of peace. Indecisive wars, in contrast, tended to produce shorter periods of peace.[2]

History

The longest periods of peace in European and world history have, in fact been those in which there was a decided imbalance in military strength in favour of a *status quo* power. The Prussian victory over France in 1870, following its victory over Austria in 1866, made clear to all that Berlin was now the capital of the strongest European country. Many Frenchmen hoped for revenge and for the opportunity to regain the lost provinces of Alsace and Lorraine but they could only do so if they could mobilise a powerful anti-German coalition. The German Chancellor, Otto von Bismarck, spent the next 19 years making sure that this would not happen. He formed alliances with his old enemy Austria-Hungary and with Russia and Italy. He also sought Britain's friendship by supporting Britain's colonial policy in Egypt and so he effectively isolated France.

Thus, there was peace in Europe from 1871 until Bismarck's dismissal in 1890. The absence of war was caused not by a balance of power but because there was an imbalance with the most powerful country supporting the *status quo*. Germany was also led by a statesman of the highest calibre who was determined to use his power to maintain peace and to avoid so offending the other European states that they formed an anti-German coalition. His achievement was all the more remarkable because until 1871 he was the epitome of the revisionist – the man who by blood and iron created a new empire out of the countries of Central Europe. Had there been an effective arms control lobby at the time, no doubt, it would have advocated the catastrophic policy of equalising French and German strength. Yet, if this policy had been followed, once France found itself in the position where it had a chance of regaining the territories lost in 1871, Europe would have been plunged again into conflict.

In the event, it was not the arms control lobby which brought about war in 1914, but the incompetence of Bismarck's successors. They made it seem that Germany was a restless, dissatisfied power and, above all, they alienated Russia and failed to dissuade it from forming an alliance with France in 1893. There had always been a danger that France and Russia would join together because France was permanently looking for an ally and Russia's interests clashed with Austria's in the Balkans. Both states wanted to dominate the new Balkan countries which were emerging from the wreckage of the Ottoman Empire. Thus, it had taken all Bismarck's skill to keep the two Eastern Empires on friendly terms. Once Bismarck fell, his successors made little effort to continue his policies. Yet their failure to do so produced a balance of power between Austria and Germany on one side and France, Russia and eventually Britain on the other. In 1914 the French, British and Russians believed that they had the strength to prevent Austria destroying Serbia and Germany dominating Belgium. The First World War was the trial of this strength.

After the end of the war, Germany was partly disarmed. As a result of this change, and because Russia was in the throes of revolution, France became the dominant military power in Europe. Unfortunately, instead of supporting France because it was the bastion of European peace and preeminently a *status quo* power, many English and American commentators did everything possible to encourage France to reduce its armed forces. The general attitude was perhaps best summed up by Sir Samuel Hoare when he wrote later,

> so sure indeed were we of the virtues of disarmament that we early became irritated with other countries and particularly with our former allies, the French, when they would not agree with us. Anti-French feeling became very strong . . . The press in and out of season clamoured for equality of status for Germany.[3]

Thus, what we would now call the arms control lobby called for equality of military power between France and Germany. Many wrongly believed that France's large army was the main cause of Franco-German friction. In fact Germany was dissatisfied with the postwar settlement in general and resented the French army only because it was the main block to its revision. The correct strategy for the democracies was, as Winston Churchill constantly pointed out, to try to reduce German political dissatisfaction whilst maintaining French military dominance. It was precisely when France lost its military dominance, without reducing German restlessness, that Europe was condemned to fight another war. Had French leaders the determination to crush Germany before the full weight of the Ruhr was placed behind the armaments drive, Europe might still have escaped with a minor conflict. But those who attacked France for its 'failure to disarm' were unlikely to support any effort it made to crush its rival and France lacked the will to carry out such a move on its own. As Colonel Heywood, the British Military Attaché in Paris, minuted in May 1933, the French were afraid of incurring the international criticisms which they had aroused when they took over the Ruhr in 1923. Furthermore, if they waited for the League of Nations to act against German rearmament, Germany would be ready for war.[4]

What was true of France in Europe was, of course, true of Britain as a world power. Whilst the British fleet remained dominant, the *status quo* could be maintained.[5] Britain's naval dominance was threatened by the growing naval might of the United States and Japan. With the USA Britain was able to come to an accommodation, albeit one that was sometimes uneasy; with Japan the long-term problems were much greater. Whilst Britain and the other European powers were fully involved in the First World War, Japan used the opportunity to try to dominate China. At that time China managed to resist most of the Japanese demands but they showed that Tokyo was likely to try to overturn the Asian *status quo* unless sufficient force could be mobilised against it. Japan's determination to control China revived during the Great Depression and Britain was no longer powerful enough on its own to deter Japanese expansionism. However, it might still have been possible for Britain and the USA acting together to thwart Tokyo's ambitions without recourse to war. It was the inability of the USA and Britain to act together which emboldened the Japanese to expand their empire. The relative decline in the power of the Royal Navy, US isolationism and European distractions weakened the power of the countries which supported the *status quo* in the Far East and paved the way for the war in the Pacific. Yet the anti-military lobby in Britain and the United States actually made the situation worse by encouraging their governments to make unilateral reductions in defence forces, whilst very often exhorting them to stand up for China against Japanese encroachments.

After the end of the Second World War, the democracies came to believe that Soviet armies were the most powerful in Europe, whilst, on their side, the Western countries had developed nuclear weapons and had used them against Japan. Both sides, therefore, feared the outbreak of war; the West because it believed that Soviet armies could overrun Europe and the Russians because they feared atomic attacks on their territory. European exhaustion, together with these fears, rather than any balance of conventional military forces, preserved an uneasy peace even though there were deep political disagreements. Outside Europe, the US and British fleets were dominant until the late 1960s and thus Soviet leaders usually avoided challenging the *status quo*, except in the most cautious and indirect manner. Moreover, when they did try to alter the balance by placing medium- and intermediate-range missiles (MRBM and IRBM) in Cuba in September 1962, the Russians were forced to back down. In the 1970s the extra-European situation became more dangerous precisely because of the growth of Soviet naval forces and the creation of a balance of naval power seemed to be combined with Soviet willingness to upset the *status quo* in an arc of countries from Afghanistan to Angola and from Ethiopia to Kampuchea.

Statesmen in Britain in particular have often talked as if they believed that a balance of power were essential if peace were to be preserved. Thus, Lord Haldane, the Lord Chancellor, told the German Ambassador in London in December 1912,

> the roots of English policy . . . lay in the opinion that was generally held that the equilibrium of the two groups [France and Russia on one side and Germany and Austria on the other] should be more or less maintained. Under no circumstances, therefore, could Britain tolerate the overthrow of the French . . . England could not afford after a French defeat to face a homogeneous Continental group under the leadership of a single power, nor did she intend to do so.[6]

Haldane's statement was interesting because Britain had watched Germany defeat France in 1871 without feeling obliged to intervene militarily, although it had offered to mediate. Moreover, Britain had been content with German dominance whilst Bismarck was Chancellor. It was the unreliability and even hostility of German policy under Kaiser William which alienated British leaders. Even so, time and again Conservative and Liberal British statesmen offered to come to terms with Germany. Their efforts were rebuffed but they hardly squared with their supposed preoccupation with the balance of power.

The demand for such a balance is very largely a rationalisation for a particular policy and a way of criticising foreign governments for their actions. It implies that statesmen had a very much better idea of the balance of military forces than they actually had. National leaders do not spend their time examining the weapons, training and numbers of foreign armies to see whether the balance of power has been upset and thus whether they ought to throw their weight on the other side. Rather they dislike the policy of another state and form an alliance with other countries which want to bring those policies to an end. In other words their fears are political not military. However, once they have formed an alliance to back their interests, they are inclined to describe any addition to the power of potential enemies as an attempt to overturn the military balance. Their policy is affected by political not military changes. Even if the West Europeans had come to the conclusion in the 1950s that the USA was stronger than the Soviet Union, they would not have joined the Warsaw Pact in order to right the balance. They supported the USA because, by and large, they approved of its policies, not because of any need to preserve a balance of power.

Nor is there anything new about this, at least as far as Britain has been concerned. In his analysis of Britain's role in world affairs since the time of Henry VIII, Lord Strang showed that British leaders often talked as if the preservation of balance were vital but acted in other ways. Thus, Henry VIII himself supported the idea of such a balance 'though he did not practise it'.[7] Subsequently statesmen and theorists believed that if states grew

> strong by violence, intervention against them would be both a right and a duty: this would be a just war. If they grew strong by marriage or inheritance . . . this would in itself give no right to take up arms: but, if such states had already shown an encroaching disposition . . . then the balancing system would authorize immediate interference to procure securities or to prevent the aggrandizement.[8]

Thus, French expansion under Louis XIV was halted by coalitions of the other states, not because of any theoretical attachment to the balance of power but because they saw the immediate threat to themselves. In the nineteenth century, when Britain itself was at the height of its power, Lord Palmerston

> did not necessarily seek the support of the weaker against the stronger, as the classic doctrine of the balance of power would normally suggest. On the contrary, his tactic was often to work with and so to seek to control, the power which for geographical or strategic reasons was in the strongest position . . .[9]

Thus, our ancestors interpreted the doctrine of balance of power much more flexibly than many have assumed; they were keenly aware of any threat to their political interests and always ready to denounce such threats as the result of an upset to the balance but they did not pursue such a balance mechanistically and for its own sake.

Professor Hedley Bull has argued that a statesman's purpose in preserving a balance of power is, in any case,

> not to preserve peace, but to preserve the system of states itself. Preservation of the balance of power requires war when this is the only means whereby the power of a potentially dominant state can be checked.[10]

Thus, the balance helps prevent 'the system from being transformed by conquest into a universal empire', as was the case with the Roman Empire. On the other hand, if modern statesmen have sought a balance of power through arms control agreements, as they have claimed to do from the Washington Conference of 1921-2 to the MBFR talks, it is clear that they did not believe that their object was to preserve the states system. The Anglo-German naval conversations before 1914 may have been implicitly designed to prevent a clash for world dominance between the leading European and the leading maritime power. But there was little threat in 1921 of the emergence of a universal empire. Britain was clearly in decline, the USA was just emerging as a world power and Japan was not yet a power of the same order. What the negotiators were trying to do was to settle the Far East and to avoid an arms race. Some might say that, by trying to prevent the emergence of an arms race, they were avoiding a competition to see which was the dominant world power. But again it is not clear that that was the way they saw it.

Some may argue that statesmen were putting an acceptable gloss on their desire to preserve the state's system by their claim that the object was to preserve peace. After all the anti-military lobby would hardly support efforts to preserve separate states, given as it is to believing with Goldsworthy Lowes Dickinson that it is the 'rivalry of all states which is the real cause of war'.[11] But this interpretation is much too Machiavellian and we now know from the diaries and papers of those involved that they were not trying to hide their real intentions. If these aims were 'Machiavellian' it was only in so far as they sought the best 'deal' for their own countries in the agreements negotiated. But everything points rather to a widespread, though false, conviction amongst the general public that a balance of power preserves peace. The conviction is not, of course, shared by the disarmament lobby which looks for the abolition of armaments, nor by the 'realists' who want to see their country militarily dominant.

The Nuclear Age

Fortunately the general obsession with equality will probably not reduce the prospects for peace in the nuclear age. However equal in size the US and Soviet nuclear forces were to become, this would not increase the prospects that either side could hope for victory in a nuclear war and any major conventional war could lead to the use of nuclear weapons. Such a victory could only be achieved if one side could totally destroy the nuclear delivery systems of the other in a surprise attack. Moreover, the nuclear stalemate affects the prospects for conventional war. Both Eastern and Western governments have tried to avoid any risks which might lead to a nuclear exchange. Contrary to popular opinion, in these very important respects nuclear weapons have made arms control agreements easier to achieve. As we shall see, equality may now sometimes serve as a guideline for the arms control negotiations, without increasing the prospects for war, as such a policy would have done in the pre-nuclear age.

The advance of technology has strengthened arms control in other ways. In the nineteenth century military preparations could quickly be undertaken. This reduced the effectiveness of agreements between states since they could rapidly be undone. Today military preparations take much longer and with every advance in technology this timelag increases. Even in the interwar period it took only a few years to design, develop and produce an aircraft. The complex aircraft of today usually take more than a decade between conception and production. Thus international agreements take longer to undo. However, there is also a possibility that military preparations may begin when relations between two countries are at their nadir but be completed when such relations have considerably improved. In these circumstances arms control agreements may sometimes help reduce suspicions that weapons are going to be used in hostile ways.[12] Such agreements will also be more easily achieved if the armaments have lost their political function.

It is extremely doubtful whether any East-West agreements were possible in the political conditions prevailing in the 1950s, however such agreements as were attempted did not strike at the roots of the military problems of the period. At that time the West was, rightly or wrongly, mainly concerned about the size of Soviet conventional forces in Europe and to a lesser extent about the size of the Soviet submarine force. Conversely, the Soviet Union was mainly worried about US nuclear weapons carried in bombers based in Britain and elsewhere. The disarmament negotiations did address these fears but in a curious and roundabout manner. For much of the time they were designed in theory to achieve the abolition of nuclear armaments and the reduction of conventional forces down to a level which was supposed to make aggression impossible.[13] It would have been more direct to try to bargain away US bases for the demobilisation of Soviet divisions and the destruction of Soviet tanks.

Proposals

The forces for bases deal was very largely blocked by the hopes for more far-reaching disarmament agreements — as so often, the best is the enemy of the good. But progress was also blocked by the obsession with equality. We should substitute for this obsession efforts to limit those military missions which appear particularly threatening. The same suggestion has been made, though for different reasons, by the former Director of the International Institute for Strategic Studies (IISS), Dr Christoph Bertram. In a paper on the *Future of Arms Control* he argued that SALT had been hampered by the pace of technological change, by the increasing difficulty of verifying agreements and by the trend towards multi-purpose weapons, such as cruise missiles, which cannot simply be categorised as strategic or tactical, nuclear or non-nuclear.[14] He suggested that the way to overcome these problems was to abandon precise numerical limits on numbers of weapons and to concentrate on efforts to limit missions which appeared destabilising. He cited as an example of the sort of agreement which he had in mind, the Anti-Ballistic Missile Treaty (ABM) associated with the first SALT agreement. Although this did specify the numbers of ABMs which the Super Powers could retain, it set the limitations so low that it effectively precluded the evolution of the mission altogether.

A further argument for attempts to limit missions rather than numbers is that, where armaments were defined by their missions in earlier agreements, these definitions have survived the ravages of time particularly well. For example, aircraft carriers are defined under the 1936 Montreux Convention, which lays down what warships can pass through the Dardanelles into or out of the Black Sea, as 'surface vessels of war, whatever their displacement, designed or adapted primarily for the purpose of carrying and operating aircraft at sea'.[15] Since the Convention was signed, aircraft and carrier design has changed drastically — both helicopters and fixed-wing aircraft have come to be used very widely at sea, whilst aircraft carriers have grown to an immense size and have now begun to shrink again with the development of fixed-wing aircraft which can take off vertically. But the definition has remained adequate through all changes.

Measures to limit missions should thus ideally restrict future as well as current technologies. Sometimes it will be clear what technologies should be restricted because their potential will be obvious; thus the threat to land-based ICBMs from accurate MIRVs is indisputable. On the other hand, some major changes in technology were by no means always obvious to contemporaries. The Washington Naval Agreement of 1921-2 very effectively limited capital ships and carrier construction but the greatest advances at the time were in the capabilities of the planes based on the carriers. By the Second World War these had made battleships obsolete in some roles. Certain commentators and naval officers appreciated the nature of the changes which were taking place but many did not and the Washington Naval Treaty had nothing to say about the most dynamic element in naval armaments.

Arms control agreements should above all be designed to ensure an NWS's ability to retaliate with nuclear weapons even if another state launched an unexpected all-out nuclear attack against it. Dr Bertram argued that, in the strategic field,

> three potential military capabilities give most cause for concern, the ability to destroy through a pre-emptive strike vulnerable land-based missiles in silos; the possibility of effective strategic anti-submarine warfare against SSBN, the major second strike launcher platforms and anti-satellite capabilities.[16]

The former Director of the IISS thus argued that it was these capabilities which should be limited by future agreements. The difficulties can hardly be exaggerated. For example, the development of anti-satellite weapons has already gone so far that it would be difficult to ensure that an agreement was being observed in peacetime. In a major war it appears unlikely that satellites could be protected by agreement because of the part they would play in reconnaissance, particularly at sea. Already in the war between Britain and Argentina in 1982, there were reports that the Americans were supplying Britain with satellite information about the whereabouts of Argentine vessels. Conversely, as the war progressed, the Soviet Union greatly improved its reconnaissance over the South Atlantic by launching further nuclear powered satellites designed for ocean surveillance. One well informed US journal commented that this sort of satellite was 'among the highest priority targets for US anti-satellite weapons systems because of the utility of the spacecraft's data in actual war-fighting situations'.[17] Nevertheless, wherever possible, arms control agreements should be used to enhance the security of the nuclear retaliatory forces.

Efforts to negotiate any important arms control agreements will only be effective if detente can be restored and based on some degree of political agreement. Short of such a rapprochement, agreements will eventually start to break down. Historical experience points in the same direction. To take one classic example, the German High Seas Fleet was developed before the First World War with the express object of fighting the Royal Navy or of frightening Britain into neutrality in the event of a European war. British statesmen tried hard to limit the Anglo-German naval race. The Germans were prepared to make such an agreement, provided Britain declared in advance that it would be neutral in the event of a European conflict.[18] In other words political detente had to precede military. Similarly Japan might have been prepared to prolong the naval arms control agreements with Britain and the USA after 1935 if the Western states had given it a free hand to dominate China. Most Western leaders were prepared during the 1960s and 1970s to accept Soviet dominance in Eastern Europe. In that area Russia was a *status quo* power. But the conviction increasingly gained ground that the Russians were behaving in a revisionist fashion in Africa, South East Asia and above all in Afghanistan. Detente and arms control will only prosper once again when some *modus vivendi* has been found by East and West in these areas.

Notes

1. 'Mitterand places France firmly in Western camp', *The Times*, 25 September 1981.
2. G. Blainey, *The Causes of War*, Sun Books, Melbourne, 1977, p. 112.
3. Sir Samuel Hoare, Viscount Templewood, *Nine Troubled Years*, Collins, London, 1954, p. 113.
4. Admiralty minute of 15 May 1933, ADM/116/2945.
5. Hoare, *Nine Troubled Years*, p. 135 passim.
6. Prince Lichnowsky, *Heading for the Abyss*, Constable, London, 1928, p. 349. See also p. 31.
7. Lord Strang, *Britain in World Affairs*, Faber & Faber and André Deutsch, London, 1961, p. 56.
8. Loc. cit., p. 69.
9. Loc. cit., p. 154.
10. Hedley Bull, *The Anarchical Society*, Macmillan, London, 1981, p. 107.
11. G. Lowes Dickinson, *War: Its Nature, Cause and Cure*, Allen and Unwin, London, 1923, p. 68.
12. See Chapter 3 on 'the political approach'.
13. For the negotiations see *The Disarmament Question 1945-1954*, Central Office of Information, London, August 1954. See also *Documents on Disarmament 1945-1959*, two vols, Department of State, Washington, 1960.
14. C. Bertram, *The Future of Arms Control*, Adelphi paper, no 146, IISS, London, 1978. I do not, of course, believe that the pace of technological change has increased as explained above.
15. The text of the Convention was reprinted in *Survival*, November/December 1976.
16. Bertram, *Future of Arms Control*.
17. 'Falklands reconnaissance improved by Soviet Union', *Aviation Week and Space Technology*, 24 May 1982.
18. H.W. Koch, *The Origins of the First World War*, Macmillan, London, 1972, p. 44.

3 THE POLITICAL APPROACH

It is suspicion, hostility and fear which lead nations to increase their armaments or to be reluctant to disarm. In the total absence of political enmities, as between say Australia and New Zealand, there is no need to arm but also no concern if one or other state does so in order to protect itself against a third party. Between potentially hostile groups in contrast it is extremely difficult to reduce suspicions. As the 1958 British defence White Paper put it, 'the Western nations and the Soviet Union face one another with deep-seated mutual mistrust. Each fears the other has aggressive intentions, and no amount of pacific assurances in both directions has so far succeeded in removing these suspicions.'[1]

The Conference on Security and Co-operation in Europe (CSCE)

But, if suspicion and fear are responsible for armaments, would it not be wiser to aim to reduce these rather than to try to limit the armaments directly? Direct arms control negotiations often become bogged down in military details, yet these could be side-stepped by negotiations on the political kernel of the dispute. The problem is that the real crux of major disputes is rarely susceptible to negotiation. The kernel of the confrontation between the Western powers and Japan in the 1930s was Japan's determination to dominate China. No amount of negotiation was likely to change this. In Europe, in contrast, great efforts were made to appease Hitler but nothing except total control over the European heartland was enough to satisfy his ambitions. The problem since 1945 has been largely ideological — the desire of the West and of the Soviet Union to see democracy and communism respectively become the prevalent ideology. There is little negotiation can do to change these ambitions though it can perhaps circumscribe the way each bloc advances its ideology and interests. This is what the CSCE was supposed to do from 1972 to 1975 and what makes the conference in many ways the most important one to be convened since 1945.

In the 1950s and 1960s the Warsaw Pact periodically suggested that a conference should be convened to settle Europe's problems, much as the Vienna conference had sorted out the problems resulting from the

33

Napoleonic Wars and the Versailles or Paris conference had concluded the First World War. The Western countries fought shy of these proposals however. They were intensely suspicious of all Soviet suggestions and they were unwilling at that period to accept any agreement giving the stamp of legality or finality to the borders imposed on Germany and the East European states at the end of the Second World War. In 1966 and again in 1967 the Russians reverted to the idea of a general conference. They suggested that it should lead to the removal of all foreign (that is US) military bases and 'recognition of the actually existing frontiers between European states'. They also called for increased co-operation between East and West on the basis of 'the principle of peaceful co-existence of states with different social systems'.[2]

The Western attitude towards such a conference began to soften following Chancellor Brandt's negotiation of treaties between the two Germanies and between West Germany and Poland from 1970 to 1972. Brandt's policy was based on the recognition that confrontation had failed to persuade the Soviet Union to disgorge East Germany and on the hope that East-West contacts would increase under a policy of detente. Building on Brandt's 'ostpolitik', NATO ministers suggested at a meeting in December 1971 that a European conference might be convened, though it

> should not serve to perpetuate the post-war division of Europe, but rather contribute to reconciliation and co-operation . . . by initiating a process of reducing the barriers that still exist.[3]

The decision to hold a conference forced Western governments and commentators to assess what could be done on the political level to improve East-West relations. What was it about the Eastern bloc which caused most concern and fear in the West? The simple answer was the whole nature of the Eastern political system; not the ownership of the means of production by the government since that is common now in the West, but the repression which went with this and the avowed aim of spreading this system around the world. The Western view of the Eastern world is naturally greatly influenced by those who have seen it at first hand. To quote two of these; Milovan Djilas, Tito's erstwhile lieutenant wrote,

> contemporary communism is that type of totalitarianism which consists of three basic factors for controlling the people. The first

is power; the second ownership; the third ideology. They are mono-
polized by the one and only political party, or . . . by a new class.
No totalitarian system in history . . . has succeeded in incorporating
simultaneously all these factors for controlling the people to this
degree.[4]

Alexander Solzhenitsyn described the whole system as a prison camp,
a 'Gulag Archipelago':

scattered from the Bering Strait almost to the Bosporous are
thousands of islands of the spellbound Archipelago. They are invisible but they exist. And the invisible slaves of the Archipelago . . .
have to be transported from island to island just as invisibly and
uninterruptedly . . . Great ports exist for this purpose — transit
prisons; and smaller ports, camp transit points.[5]

The essence of such a system could not be changed from the outside
or overnight. Indeed a sudden change, amounting to a convulsion, in
one of the Super Powers might bring unimagined disaster. But the
Kremlin might be persuaded, in return for Western concessions, to pay
lip-service to human rights, to tolerance, to free speech, to freedom of
religion and to the liberty of peoples to move about within their own
countries and across frontiers unhindered. Once they had admitted the
value of such rights, might they not also gradually be persuaded into
permitting greater freedom in Eastern Europe, if not in the Soviet
Union itself? If such changes were made then Western fears would
decline of their own accord and with them Western armaments. Of
course, there are many who would argue that such a programme is
totally unrealistic. Solzhenitsyn himself would maintain that it betrays
unrealistic liberal hopes of the way that the Soviet Union might
develop. But once the possibility of convening a conference began to be
discussed, the West was bound to ask itself what it most feared about
the Eastern bloc and equally inevitably it was bound to answer in
the way that it did. As long as the Berlin wall exists, as long as the
whole Iron Curtain is not only maintained but gradually improved — so
that anyone attempting to cross it will be either shot down by newly-
installed automatic weapons or blown up by newly-sown mines — so
long the divisions of Europe and the fears which go with it will never
be removed. But the West could not ask for the dismantling of the
barriers in one move. It had to approach its object with some circum-
spection, for the advances in human rights which reassured the West

were precisely what gave the East most concern.

Western governments were to argue that suspicion and fear between East and West were the result of secrecy, lack of cultural contacts and of the suppression of human rights. Much as the nineteenth-century Liberals, Richard Cobden and John Bright would have done, they contended that the more contact there was between states and peoples at all levels, the less chance there would be of frictions and suspicions leading to war. The East Europeans argued that capitalism or imperialism was at the root of East-West suspicions but that these suspicions could be reduced by the acceptance of the frontiers established since 1945.

The Negotiations

Despite the contrasting motives of the Western and Warsaw Pact powers for holding the conference, preparatory talks began in Helsinki in November 1972 and lasted until July 1973. They were attended by representatives of 33 European countries, including Luxemburg and the Vatican but excluding Albania. The Albanians shared the fear of the Chinese that the conference would simply direct Soviet expansion eastwards. The USA and Canada also attended. The preparatory talks ended with a foreign ministers' meeting in July 1973. By that time there was agreement that the agenda should be divided into 'baskets' on security, economic and technical co-operation, human rights and contacts, and arrangements for succeeding conferences. But there was only limited agreement on what should go into these baskets and when the foreign ministers spoke they tended to retract some of the concessions previously made by their delegates.

Not surprisingly, when the negotiations began in earnest, agreement was by no means guaranteed. In the first section or basket 1 the East Europeans wanted frontiers to be declared 'immutable'. But West Germany, Spain and Ireland hoped to change their frontiers peacefully and opposed the use of this word. Eventually delegates reached agreement that 'frontiers can be changed, in accordance with international law, by peaceful means and by agreement'.[6] Principle 111 of basket 1 refers to frontiers as 'inviolable' rather than 'immutable'. The Russians also wanted the principle of non-intervention in other states to apply only to interference in states with different social systems, that is to interference by capitalist states in socialist ones. However, in order to achieve their other aims at the conference, the

Russians were forced to agree that all the principles applied 'irrespective of [states'] political, economic or social systems'. Western delegates hoped that this might slightly reduce the likelihood that the Russians would intervene in one of the East European countries in the way that they had intervened in Hungary in 1956 and Czechoslovakia in 1968. But the Soviet government has always maintained that it was asked for help on these occasions. At a press briefing held in Helsinki during the foreign ministers' conference in 1973, a Soviet spokesman said in answer to a question, 'that the Czechoslovak government had requested assistance in 1968 so that there had been no intervention. After ten minutes of questions like [this] he hurriedly closed the press conference'.[7]

Potentially even more dramatic in its influence, in the unlikely event of it greatly influencing Soviet policy, was Western insistence on more frequent contacts between people in the East and West and greater respect for human rights in all countries. The Russians would have liked to restrict East-West contacts to trade and technical exchanges so that they could benefit from Western scientific advances without being 'contaminated' by outside ideas. However, in order to obtain the technical benefits they wanted, they had to accept clauses in the Final Act of the conference calling for increased respect for human rights. In basket 111 states undertake 'to facilitate freer movement and contacts, individually, collectively, whether privately or officially, among persons, institutions and organizations'. The distinctions were important because the Soviet Union wanted to restrict exchanges to official delegations. The participating states also agreed that their governments should 'improve conditions under which journalists from one participating state exercise their profession in other participating states'. Above all there was agreed in basket 1 that,

> the participating States will respect human rights and fundamental freedoms, including the freedom of thought, conscience, religion or belief, for all without distinction as to race, sex, language or religion. They will promote and encourage the effective exercise of civil, political, economic, social, cultural and other rights and freedoms all of which derive from the inherent dignity of the human person . . .

The threats which these clauses theoretically represent to the Soviet political system are obvious, although of course they have subscribed to earlier declarations of this sort which they have subsequently ignored.[8]

Implications for the Soviet Bloc

The present Soviet and East European political system could not
survive any great reduction in the secrecy surrounding its activities, any
far-reaching emphasis on human rights, or indeed any extensive opening
of Soviet society to the world outside. Thus, the Russians immediately
set out to prevent the Final Act from being used to undermine socialist
'unity'. As Mr Brezhnev himself put it: 'no the socialist system is not a
"closed society", we are open to everything that is truthful and honest
. . . but our doors will always be closed to publications propagandising
war, violence, racism and hatred'.[9]

Soviet writers poured scorn on the idea that increased contacts
would bring peace or that the two world wars would have been
prevented if there had been more tourism or exchanges of information.
In this they were undoubtedly correct.[10] The Second World War was
caused by the Axis powers' determination to dominate Europe and Asia
and not by lack of information about these intentions. On the other
hand, the Soviet Union is even more secretive than the Germans and
Japanese were in the 1930s and its very furtiveness enhances Western
suspicions about its intentions. It might be that agreements could be
negotiated or compromises reached on some issues affecting East-West
relations, but that this is prevented by Soviet secrecy. Whatever the
merits of the argument, in the event the East Europeans were persuaded
to accept the proposition that 'the development of contact [is] an
important element in the strengthening of friendly relations and trust
among peoples'.

They also reluctantly accepted the basket 111 undertaking to permit
freer dissemination of books. In practice they have increased the
number of Western books and articles circulated in the Soviet Union
but they have made certain that these deal with technical or historical
subjects which do not threaten their own power.[11] Thus, on the one
hand, they prevented copies of Dr Kissinger's memoirs being displayed
at the Third Moscow book fair in September 1981. On the other hand,
the chairman of the USSR state committee for publishing boasted,

> the USSR increases the publication of translated literature and the
> sales in the USSR of books published in other countries every year.
> According to UNESCO the Soviet Union currently holds the leading
> position in the world in publishing translated literature.[12]

Since the Final Act was signed by heads of state and government in

August 1975 there have been two conferences to review its working and operation. The first was held in Belgrade from 1977 to 1978 and the second in Madrid from 1980 to 1982. On both occasions Western delegates criticised the Soviet Union for failing to uphold the principles on human rights laid down in the Final Act and Western newspapers encouraged them to take a firm line.[13] Soviet reaction was predictable. Mr Brezhnev had warned in March 1977 that he would not accept attempts to 'undermine our socialist society'.[14] He was particularly offended by the emphasis placed on human rights in general and the rights of Soviet dissidents in particular by the Carter administration. Such dissidents he said were 'outcasts' against whom it was a 'holy duty' to protect the Soviet people. In the light of the threat to the whole CSCE process which the deadlock on human rights produced, were Western criticisms too strong? After all few can have expected the Russians to live up to all the principles. Had they done this would have been the greatest transformation in Soviet society since 1917, perhaps the greatest transformation in Russian history. In the circumstances it might have been tactically wiser and more effective to push human rights more cautiously and less publicly.

On their side the East Europeans have never admitted that they fear the effects of an open battle of words between East and West. After the Final Act was signed, some East European leaders even argued that it would increase the prospects for revolution outside the communist bloc. Hence, the East German leader, Mr Honecker, declared on 11 September 1975 that the CSCE would provide 'more favourable prospects of world-wide revolutionary progress'. He also argued that one of the most important features of any Marxist-Leninist party was its 'irreconcilable stand towards every capitalist society'.[15] Yet East European leaders never accepted the free battle for men's minds which the CSCE seemed to promise.[16] Moreover, there are many in the West who point to the dangers to peace which a defeat for the East in such a battle could bring. Professor M.E. Howard has described these people as

'minimalists', especially in official positions in Western Europe for whom friendly relations between states is an end in itself. Many of them indeed would be reluctant to see detente go any further, since the destabilisation which it might cause in the Soviet bloc could result in at best a repressive backlash from the regime and at worst in renewed international crises with the attendant risk of war.[17]

There are plenty of examples from earlier times of regimes which tried to solve their internal problems by military successes abroad. Some of the ministers who refused to make concessions to Japan and so pushed Russia into the disastrous Russo-Japanese War of 1904-5 did so in the hope that success in Manchuria would reduce criticisms of the government at home. Similarly, the Austro-Hungarian government decided to take the opportunity to crush Serbia in 1914 because it was frightened of the effects of Slav nationalism on its own peoples. Thus, a Soviet government which saw its East European bulwark crumbling and rising dissent in its non-Russian minorities might be tempted into adventures abroad. Many would argue that it intervened in Afghanistan in December 1979 because it was afraid that a fundamentalist Moslem regime might appear there, akin to the regime which had replaced the Shah in Iran in February of the same year, and that this might cause disaffection amongst the Moslems in southern Russia.

Against these dangers must be weighed the general 'liberal' assumption that human rights, democracy and peace are in some way linked together. Some analysts would deny that this is so or that the propensity to fight is affected by the nature of a state's government. They would argue that dictatorships, monarchies, democracies and oligarchies have all shown themselves willing to fight in order to expand their territories. Others would argue that it is the democracies which have been most active in local wars since 1945.[18] On the other hand, no two liberal democracies have so far gone to war with each other in the twentieth century and, if the West Europeans have been active in wars in the Third World since 1945, it is largely because of their residual colonial commitments. Conversely, there has been a series of wars between the communist states. The Soviet Union invaded Hungary in 1956 and Czechoslovakia in 1968; China and the USSR have frequently been on the brink of war and their troops actually killed each other in the 1960s; Vietnam has invaded the communist state of Kampuchea and, in retaliation, China invaded Vietnam; the Soviet Union invaded Afghanistan and became involved in a prolonged guerrilla war to depose one communist government and impose another of its own choice. All these conflicts stemmed from ideological feuds peculiar to the communist system in much the same way as religion inspired the wars which devastated post-Reformation Europe. In the long run liberalisation may make the communists less susceptible to this sort of ideological feuding, just as it has decreased the frequency of European religious wars. Moreover, the 'liberal' argument makes sense in terms of arms control. The primary technical or non-political brake on arms control agreements since 1945 has been, as we will see, the unwillingness of the Soviet Union to permit inspection on its territories.[19] These factors have to be set against the fears of the 'minimalists'.

At the other extreme are those who argue that the West should attempt to improve conditions for the East Europeans whatever the consequences. Admittedly, in the long run, the hope must be that the most unpleasant features of the communist system become a relic of the past, but the avoidance of war must surely take precedence over human rights. It would be of small consolation to the Czechs or Poles if they were to acquire the most far-reaching political liberties at the price of the obliteration of all or part of their territories. Within this limitation we do have a duty to bring justice to those within the communist bloc and this is another argument in favour of the CSCE. If the Final Act deserves our support, as I believe it does, it is because, combined with dissident pressures in Eastern Europe, it may gradually reduce the worst features of communist totalitarianism and this hope outweighs the danger of destabilised communist regimes lashing out in unpredictable directions.

Those who negotiated the agreement tried to make unpredictable military actions marginally less likely by the introduction of CBMs in the Final Act. These were not disarmament measures as such, but they were intended to reduce military secrecy and the fears that such secrecy engenders by giving advance warning of troop movements and manoeuvres and encouraging exchanges and visits between Eastern and Western armed forces. Although they were not so difficult as the discussions on human rights, the negotiations on CBMs in basket 1 encountered objections from the Soviet Union because of its obsession with secrecy. The USA was also unenthusiastic about CBMs in the early days of the negotiations.[20] The British argued that states should give 60 days advance notice of military movements or manoeuvres. The Russians countered with a proposal for five days warning of manoeuvres alone. The West Europeans wanted the whole of Europe as far as the Urals covered, the Russians wanted CBMs only to apply to frontier areas. In the end compromise was achieved. The 35 participating states agreed to give not less than 21 days advance notice of manoeuvres involving 25,000 troops within 155 miles of a frontier facing or shared with another European participating state. The participants can also notify smaller manoeuvres and major military movements and they undertake to invite observers to manoeuvres 'on a voluntary and bilateral basis'. Both sides have made some efforts to abide by this agreement. For example, the US State Department reported that in 1979 NATO states notified two large and three small-scale manoeuvres. Conversely, the Russians notified one large manoeuvre, the Hungarians one small and two of the neutrals, Switzerland and Austria, also notified large-scale manoeuvres. Observers were invited to two of the NATO manoeuvres, as well as to the Soviet manoeuvre. US representatives declined to attend and the State Department claimed that 'observers who did attend were shown demonstrations rather than exercise activity, thereby making this of questionable value in implementing the Final Act.'[21]

At the two review conferences held since 1975 the West tried to extend the CBM process. Western delegates suggested that smaller manoeuvres and movements should also be notified and that a wider area should be covered. The East Europeans countered with a proposal for a ban on all manoeuvres above a certain size, a proposal which the NATO countries said would affect them unfairly because of their need to practise co-operation between a large number of armies. At the Madrid conference the Western states tried again to persuade the Russians to accept CBMs covering the whole of Europe. The Russians replied that this was unreasonable since the USA would not have to apply CBMs to the forces it maintains on the other side of the Atlantic. US delegates responded in turn that the Russians had twice as many troops east of the Urals, which would not be covered by CBMs, as the United States had in continental USA. However, to meet East European objections, the West accepted a neutral proposal that CBMs should also cover air and naval movements off Europe's Atlantic coast. Nevertheless, this did not satisfy the Soviet Union which proposed that CBMs should cover the whole of Europe 'with the adjoining sea (ocean) areas of corresponding width'. This, as the Canadian delegate pointed out, would mean that the whole of the northern hemisphere would be covered except for Asiatic Russia and the northern part of the Pacific Ocean.[22] And so the arguments continued.

Few would argue that the CBM process has yet produced much confidence. In so far as the Russians have sometimes applied the Act's provisions half-heartedly, the agreement may actually have increased East-West frictions. In September 1981 the State Department complained that the Russians had not notified fully a manoeuvre by 100,000 men north and east of Poland:

the overall Soviet record raises deep concern about the seriousness of the Soviet Union's commitment to implement fully the Helsinki Final Act. It is now clear that the Soviet Union has failed to observe fully the Helsinki Final Act provision on prior notification of major military manoeuvres.[23]

The persistence of Soviet manoeuvres round the Polish frontiers when the trades union movement, Solidarity, campaigned for greater freedom in Poland in 1981, showed that such manoeuvres can still be used to threaten other states. It also reduced the warning that the Poles would have of impending invasion since the manoeuvres could have turned at any stage into a full-scale attack. So far the CBM process therefore remains unproven. Yet it is certainly worth pursuing. Unlike the principles on human rights, it cannot be seen as a threat to either side unless the very act of building confidence is itself suspect.

Implications for the West

The threat to the West posed by the CSCE is very different from the threat to the East. The West will not be destabilised by communist propaganda, nor will its institutions be threatened by East-West contacts. The more Western citizens visit the East European countries, the more they will see the merits of their own societies. Communist newspapers, such as the *Morning Star*, already exist in the West and the works of Mr Brezhnev are freely available to those rare individuals who want to buy and read them.

Thus, those who opposed the Final Act in the West did so because they objected to any measure which appeared to sanctify the *status quo* in Eastern Europe and because they believed that Western suspicions of Soviet intentions were justified and should not be reduced by 'artificial' agreements. As the historian Edward Crankshaw put it,

> Russia has not recanted its open declaration of ideological warfare . . . it means no holds barred in strengthening subversive movements wherever they can be found and controlled . . . In so far as Helsinki helped to dress up a hostile Power in a cloak of respectability, it was not only a betrayal of the victims of oppression, it was self-betrayal too.[24]

Some Western newspapers voiced similar fears. When the Helsinki process began, *The Times* warned,

> Soviet intentions must be judged according to actions not words.

Russians tend to believe that good relations consist of newspapers writing nice words . . . The West must point out how difficult it is to reconcile the Soviet Union's declared policies with the massive accumulation of armed forces in Eastern Europe which far outweigh Nato forces in Western Europe.[25]

The *Daily Telegraph*'s editorial voiced fears that 'Soviet communists regard [CSCE] as an important step in their long-term strategy for disarming Europe by first inducing a spirit of neutralism'. A view echoed by the expert on Soviet affairs, Leonard Schapiro.[26]

No doubt such concerns were increased by the attitudes taken by the *Morning Star* and left wing Labour Members of Parliament. Immediately after the Final Act was signed, Mr Frank Allaun called for a £1,300 million reduction in British defence spending each year. He also complained that 'all the assumptions of the cold war and military confrontation still dominate our policies, even though we are in an era of East-West detente'.[27] The *Morning Star* opened its columns to Vadim Nekrasov, a former deputy editor of *Pravda*, who criticised 'the attempts of influential Western circles to substitute a downright ideological war for an ideological struggle, inevitable in the conditions of opposing social systems existing in the world'.[28]

Against the views of such commentators as Schapiro and Crankshaw, some would argue that governments and military men are always too distrustful of their potential enemies. George Kennan has criticised those 'military planners whose professional obligation it is to set up a planner's dummy of any possible military opponent'.[29] Yet it is certainly not possible to say that military men are invariably too suspicious. To take just one example, throughout the 1930s the Royal Navy tried to play down the menace presented by German revisionism as symbolised by the growth of German naval power. Looking back at the period a modern naval historian has written:

the Director of Naval Intelligence [subsequently] pointed out that no one wanted to believe . . . that German projects were indeed a threat to British maritime security. 'The Naval Staff', he wrote, 'were not inclined to accept anything "awkward" from Naval Intelligence Division . . . It was evident that . . . no one was prepared politically to handle the resultant accusations'.[30]

It is simply not possible therefore to argue that military men are always over-cautious or that governments are always too suspicious. If the

Soviet Union is expansionist and yet our confidence in its intentions increases, because of such agreements as the Final Act, then we may reduce our armaments to a level where, even in the nuclear age, the Kremlin might be tempted into hazardous adventures. The experience of the 1970s was that, if the Soviet Union's defence policy was affected by detente, it was much less affected than that of the West. Nor is this very surprising. Western electorates wish to seize any opportunity to increase expenditure on welfare rather than armaments. There is no similar pressure in the Soviet Union, though economic problems might one day push the Soviet leaders some way in the same direction.

The long-term aim must be to convert present hostility into mutual tolerance and forbearance, just as US-Chinese suspicions have been partly overcome. But the achievement of such tolerance can hardly be easy. The attacks which the Soviet Union has made on NATO plans to deploy new weapons in Europe and the encouragement which it gives to Western unilateralism, have increased suspicions. The exiled Soviet dissident, Vladimir Bukovsky, wrote of the pacifist movement in the West in *The Times* on 4 December 1981,

> it probably consists of an odd mixture of communists, fellow travellers, muddle-headed intellectuals, hypocrites seeking popularity . . . But there is no doubt that this motley crowd is governed by a handful of scoundrels, instructed directly from Moscow.

This reaction interestingly parallels Soviet reactions to dissidents like Bukovsky himself and the support which the West extends to them.

Thus, the Russians tried to concentrate attention at the Madrid review conference on disarmament, whilst the West tried to concentrate on human rights and CBMs. Western delegates felt that 'the Soviet proposal for a conference on military detente and disarmament [was] a propaganda exercise designed to lull Western public opinion into a false sense of security'. The British delegation in particular argued that the Russians were 'more interested in creating a false sense of security in other peoples than in allowing their own people to know the true burden of their own armaments expenditures'.[31] It is notable, of course, that dissident groups in the Eastern bloc have generally demanded human rights, whilst dissident groups in the West demand disarmament. Western unilateralists have argued that a disarmament movement could be created in the East. But the East Europeans have to have human rights before they can look for disarmament, they have to have a degree of democracy before they can hope to influence their governments.

Conclusion

Surprisingly enough the CSCE process has enhanced the existing strengths and weaknesses of the two sides. Reviewing the 'hopes of Helsinki' on 3 July 1973, *The Times* claimed 'the Warsaw Pact may be stronger militarily but it is weaker politically and economically'. This remains the case and the more the Helsinki process advances the more the differences may increase. Further East-West trade may help the Soviet consumer to begin to catch up with his Western counterpart but, even after the recurrent oil crises, the West remains far ahead. On the other hand, the more East-West cultural contacts take place, the greater will be the erosion of the authoritarianism of the Eastern bloc — as events demonstrated in Poland in 1980 and 1981. On the Western side the hopes provoked by detente may deepen divisions and increase unilateralism and neutralism. If these movements have any influence on policy, as history suggests they will, then they may also enhance Soviet military superiority over the West.

The worst this could produce would be a decision by the Soviet leaders that they could only keep their empire together by adventurism abroad. Some would argue that this has already been demonstrated by Soviet support for Cuban activities in Africa and by the invasion of Afghanistan. Against these activities must be set Soviet caution over Poland in 1981. The Poles were as critical of socialist orthodoxy as the Czechs were in 1968, yet the Russians did not immediately invade. Moreover, the temptation to do so must have been considerable. The Russians have their own domino theory and they were well aware that Polish independence could have its effects on the other East European countries, if not on the Estonians, Lithuanians and Latvians within their own frontiers. The Russians responded to events in Poland by threats and criticism but they evidently hesitated before using force, which is the most that the negotiators in Helsinki can have hoped that they would do. At some stage the Russian leaders may decide that, despite the risks of nuclear war, adventurism abroad may help their internal policies but that stage has not been reached yet as far as Europe is concerned.

Nevertheless, just as arms control must be built on political detente, so the dangers of Soviet adventurism outside Europe and of Western military weakness show that the Helsinki process must be supplemented either by a large and politically divisive increase in Western military strength or by further political and military agreements. Whatever the Soviet motives for advancing disarmament proposals, the West must respond by putting forward stabilising and verifiable measures. It is more profound to tackle the causes of fear and suspicion rather than the armaments which they in turn give rise to but the two processes should not be allowed to drift too far apart. Otherwise, in the face of Soviet instability and hence unpredictability, Western governments may reduce their forces to dangerously low levels.

Notes

1. *Report on Defence 1958* Cmnd 363, para 2.
2. 'The historical importance of the Helsinki Final Act', *The Times*, 7 November 1980.
3. Ibid.
4. Milovan Djilas, *The New Class, An Analysis of the Communist System*, Thames and Hudson, London, 1957, p. 166.
5. Alexander Solzhenitsyn, *The Gulag Archipelago 1918-1956*, Collins/ Fontana, 1975, p. 489. See also *Shipwreck of a Generation, the Memoirs of Joseph Berger*, Harvill, London, 1971.
6. *Conference on Security and Co-operation in Europe, Final Act*, presented to Parliament, August 1975, Cmnd 6198, p. 3. The agreement was taken very seriously by Western statesmen, see Harold Wilson, *Final Term*, Weidenfeld and Nicolson and Michael Joseph, London, 1979, particularly p. 152 passim.
7. 'Russians put controversial gloss on the declaration of principles at Helsinki conference', *The Times*, 5 July 1973.
8. For Solzhenitsyn's views on East-West relations see 'Two years in the West', *Listener*, 4 March 1976.
9. Quoted in A. Valentinov, 'one year after Helsinki', *International Affairs*, Moscow, September 1976.
10. 'Russians oppose further contacts', *The Times*, 25 April 1974.
11. Wolfgang Winter, 'the CSCE basket three; who is going to fill it?' *Aussen Politik*, no 4, 1976.
12. Boris Stukalin, 'Moscow book fair', *Soviet News*, 1 September 1981.
13. 'Stand firm in Belgrade', *The Times*, 1 August 1977.
14. 'Mr Brezhnev accuses US of interference', *The Times*, 22 March 1977.
15. *Neues, Deutschland*, 12 September 1975.
16. Hugh Ragsdale, ' "Detente", a semantic post mortem', *Encounter*, September 1981.
17. Michael Howard, 'Helsinki reconsidered', *Round Table*, July 1977.
18. Istvan Kende, '116 wars in 30 years', D. Carlton and C. Schaerf (eds.), *Arms Control and Technological Innovation*, Croom Helm, London, 1977.
19. *Documents on Disarmament 1945-59*, vol. 1, pp. 278 and 467.
20. Victor-Yves Ghebali, 'les mesures de confiance d'Helsinki', *Defense Nationale*, April 1977.
21. 'Implementation of Helsinki Accord', June-November 1979, US Department of State, Washington, pp. 8-9.
22. 'Security conference bogged down again', *The Times*, 21 July 1981.

23. 'US accuses Moscow of violating agreement', *The Times*, 9 September 1981.

24. E. Crankshaw, 'Why the West may live to regret Helsinki', *Observer*, 3 August 1975.

25. 'The Hopes at Helsinki', *The Times*, 3 July 1973.

26. L. Schapiro, 'Soviet strategy at Helsinki', *Daily Telegraph*, 12 August 1975.

27. 'After Helsinki cut arms, Cabinet told', *Morning Star*, 7 August 1975.

28. V. Nekrasov, 'Helsinki balance sheet one year after', *Morning Star*, 10 August 1976.

29. G.F. Kennon, 'A Last Warning', *Encounter*, July 1978.

30. G. Till in Philip Towle (ed.), *Estimating Foreign Military Power*, Croom Helm, London, 1982, p. 185.

31. 'Britain is shocked by Soviet tactics', *The Times*, 3 February 1981.

4 THE HUMANITARIAN APPROACH

Introduction

Given the difficulty of avoiding wars by arms control measures, some would argue that we should accept that wars will occur and concentrate our attention on trying to reduce the destructiveness of military conflict by restricting the use of certain weapons. This suggestion frequently produces wry smiles on the faces of both hard-headed realists and pacifists. The pacifists argue that war is so horrible that fighting should never take place. They also argue that if the use of some weapons is said to be illegitimate this implies that the use of others is legitimate or even desirable. The realists argue that the more horrible war is, the less often it will break out and, in any case, deny the idea that 'some well intentioned body in Geneva could succeed in drawing up a set of rules for war after the fashion of a football game, specifying what weapons may be used'.[1] Yet the Laws of War, which impose some limits on combatants, are of long standing.

The 1907 Hague Peace Conference laid down that 'prisoners of war . . . must be humanely treated . . . (and) shall be treated as regards rations, quarters and clothing on the same footing as the troops of the government which captured them'. The same conference distinguished between combatants and non-combatants and consequently prohibited 'attack on bombardment, by whatever means, of towns, villages, dwellings or buildings which are undefended'.[2] It also banned the pillaging or the confiscation of private property. Of course such rules have by no means always been obeyed. The distinction between combatants and non-combatants was a product of nineteenth-century conditions and the lack of really deep religious and ideological divisions between nations. In the age of total wars when, as in the two world wars or in guerrilla and civil conflicts, the whole population is involved in the war effort, the distinction starts to break down. In the Second World War the treatment of prisoners of war on the Eastern Front was deplorable. However, in other cases prisoners have been well treated and the laws governing their handling have been scrupulously observed. Much depends upon the character of the states involved.

History

There were attempts to humanise warfare by limiting the types of weapons and the methods of waging war in the Middle Ages. Indeed it might be said to be the original type of arms control. But the modern history of such efforts begins with the St Petersburg Conference in 1868. The Conference banned the use of exploding bullets in wars fought between the parties to the agreement. The First Hague Peace Conference followed this up in 1899 with a ban on expanding bullets. The difference between the two types of ammunition was that exploding bullets contained gunpowder or other explosives, just as artillery shells do, whereas expanding bullets were designed to break up when they hit people and to cause extensive wounds. The 1899 Conference also banned the use of projectiles, 'the sole object of which is the diffusion of asphyxiating or deleterious gases'.[3] In other words it attempted to prevent poisonous gases being used in warfare.

The limitations on the use of exploding and expanding bullets held up fairly well for a time, although some would argue that modern small-calibre high-velocity rifle bullets are just as destructive. On the other hand, the ban on the use of gas-filled projectiles collapsed altogether during the First World War. The French began to use projectiles containing ethyl bromo-acetate, which they claimed was intended to irritate rather than to injure enemy soldiers and, partly because the projectiles used were quite small, their claims appear to have been correct.[4] However, this initial use, together with the general pressure on nations fighting for their survival and frustrated by their inability to break the stalemate of the trenches, helped to erode the 1899 agreement. The Germans released 150 tons of chlorine gas from 6,000 cylinders at Ypres on 22 April 1915.[5] They could argue that they were not breaking any agreement since the 1899 Conference had banned the use of gas-filled projectiles, not cylinders, but their action effectively removed all inhibitions on the use of poisonous gas.

To try to prevent a repetition of this escalation, the Geneva Protocol was drawn up in 1925. It reaffirmed the ban on the 'use of asphyxiating, poisonous or other gases, and of all analogous liquids, materials or devices'. The Geneva Protocol was breached by the Italians during the invasion of Abyssinia in 1935.[6] However, lethal gases were not used by the major combatants during the Second World War. The reasons for this were a source of some dispute between Western and Soviet delegates to the disarmament negotiations in the 1950s. Western spokesmen argued that it was a simple case of deterrence and that, if the history of the last half century teaches us anything, it teaches us that aggressor states, which start wars in violation of their treaty obligations, cannot be trusted to keep their paper promises regarding the methods of waging wars, if they find that the keeping of those promises stands in the way of their accomplishing their aggressive designs.[7]

Soviet spokesmen placed more emphasis on the role played by the Geneva Protocol in preventing the use of gas. They were anxious at that time to play down the importance of deterrence though, after Hitler's treatment of the Nazi-Soviet Pact, they can hardly have had much real faith in Nazi respect for treaties. Recently, Soviet writers appear to have come round to the Western view. Major General Kozlov wrote in August 1979, 'the fear of retribution prevented the Nazi aggressors from using toxic agents in the course of the Second World War although intensive preparations were made'.[8] In fact the general conclusion to be derived from this history of non-use agreements is that, unfortunately, they may break down in warfare if the incentive to breach them is strong enough.

Postwar Developments

The war in Vietnam once more aroused interest in non-use agreements after many years in which arms control negotiations had concentrated on attempts to reduce force levels or to stabilise military relationships. The belief gained ground, particularly amongst Third World countries, that the USA was using its technological superiority to terrorise the population of Vietnam into submission and was coldbloodedly testing its new conventional weapons on defenceless people. The use of napalm was singled out for particular criticism; 'once napalm had been introduced into the conflict, there were no effective barriers against an escalation to the most cruel and indiscriminate way of its use'.[9] People all over the world watched pictures on their television screens of women, children and other non-combatants suffering from napalm burns and pressure began to build up at the UN for the prohibition of the use of incendiary weapons in warfare. The possibility was first extensively discussed at the International Conference on Human Rights which was held in Teheran in 1968. In 1971 the UN General Assembly requested the Secretary General to produce a report on napalm. The report concluded that the General Assembly should work for the prohibition of napalm and other incendiary weapons because 'when judged against what is required to put a soldier out of military action, much of the injury caused by incendiary weapons is therefore likely to be superfluous. In terms of damage to the civilian population, incendiaries are particularly cruel in their effects'.[10] Three years later the General assembly voted to condemn the use of incendiaries, although the NATO and Warsaw Pact nations abstained on the resolution.

Already in 1973 the International Committee of the Red Cross had convened a group of experts to consider what weapons 'may cause unnecessary suffering or have indiscriminate effects'. This phraseology and the concepts behind it were derived from the St Petersburg Conference of 1868 and the two Hague Peace Conferences which, however vague their language, still provided the main basis for deciding what weapons should be used in war. The 1973 conference and its successors revealed how little systematic research had been done on the wounding effects of weapons and how few experts there were on the subject. For example, ballistics had concentrated mainly on the progress of the bullet through the barrel of the gun and through the air, and interest in the relationship between weapons and the wounds which they produced had been spasmodic and generally unscientific. Few states had experts to speak on the subject and many had already committed themselves to a view on the desirability of banning a particular weapon before they came to consider any evidence on whether it caused 'unnecessary suffering'. The committee which examined the problem (the so-called Ad Hoc Committee of the Diplomatic Conference on Humanitarian Law) therefore came to be divided on political rather than on technical lines. On the one side, the developed states had particular weapons in their armouries and wished to keep them and use them if necessary; on the other side, the developing states feared the use of such weapons against them or against guerrillas fighting the colonial powers and therefore wished to inhibit their use as much as possible.

There was nothing new in the lack of scientific evidence. No evidence had been presented to the St Petersburg Conference in 1868 to show that exploding bullets were particularly inhumane, and the evidence on expanding bullets which was put before the 1899 Hague Conference had been distorted to embarrass the British. Experiments had been carried out at Tubingen in 1898 which were believed to show that the bullets being produced by the British at Dum Dum in India were particularly inhumane because they expanded or flattened easily in the human body. However the Tubingen experiments had been

carried out with lead-fronted Mausers, which had a much larger part of
the core uncovered than those manufactured at Dum Dum and thus
produced much greater wounds. A further series of experiments com-
paring the two weapons was carried out at the University of Aberdeen
and these showed that the Mauser bullet 'produces a wound severe
beyond all proportion as compared with the Dum Dum'.[11] It is perhaps
symbolic of the unscientific nature of the subject that expanding
bullets should often still be referred to as Dum Dums and that many
modern commentators should still write as if they were unaware of the
way the evidence was misused in 1899.

It is of course easy to argue that modern conferences on weaponry
are based upon a fundamental misconception about the effect of progress in weaponry on the production of casualties in wartime. The trend
over many centuries has been for the proportion of casualties to combatants to decline. This, as the British War Office pointed out in 1899,
is easy to explain; 'in ancient times the decisive period of the combat
was the fighting hand to hand with sword or spear, which terminated
with one side or the other giving way'. Then the fugitives would be cut
down and the casualties amongst the losers would be many times as
great as the casualties amongst the victors. However, in modern times,
'the combatants are forced to keep at a more respectful distance from
one another and to employ every tactical artifice to lessen their own
losses and increase those of their opponents'.[12] According to some
figures, eight and a half million men died in the First World War but
this horrifying total was the product primarily of civilian transport
technology not weaponry. Roads and railways enabled millions of men
to be transported to the battlefield and fed there for four years. Had
the combatants been armed with swords and shields to be used in hand-
to-hand combat rather than with machine guns and artillery, millions
would have died on the first day of battle. Modern weapons prolonged
the combat and prevented the combatants coming to grips with each
other.

'Progress' since 1918 has also meant that a smaller and smaller proportion of an army is actually deployed on the battlefield. A much
greater number is now involved in the logistic tail without which the
highly complex aircraft, tanks and ships could not be moved to the
battlefield and employed effectively. Conventional warfare becomes
increasingly a battle between rival technologies fought between small
numbers of highly trained men. This was nicely illustrated by the war
between Argentina and Britain in the spring of 1982. Argentine aircraft sank four British warships. Most of the crews from the ships man-

aged to escape but the Argentines had succeeded in their aims. The targets were the ships, not the men within them and, once they had been sunk, the men were of little further use in the war.

Improvements in medical care have also helped to reduce battle casualties and disease is no longer as great a menace to an army as the enemy's forces. With proper medical care, a soldier's chances of surviving serious wounds in all parts of the body except the head have greatly improved over the last 100 years.[13] Similarly those countries which can afford to evacuate casualties rapidly by helicopter have also managed to reduce their losses in battle. All this may produce a considerable difference in the proportion of mortalities amongst the wounded of advanced states and the proportion in armies belonging to the developing nations or to guerrilla forces. Most wars since 1945 have taken place in the Third World and have often been between developing nations; improvements in medicine may therefore have had a more limited effect on the reduction of casualties than they would have had if the wars had primarily involved the developed nations. However, the crucial issue as far as the number of casualties, and particularly the number of civilian casualties, is concerned is often the location of the fighting. A battle fought in the streets of Stalingrad, Warsaw or Beirut is terribly destructive whatever the weapons employed.

None of this invalidates efforts to reduce the destructiveness of warfare through non-use agreements. The problem is to find criteria for deciding which weapons should be outlawed and ways of making agreements stand up to the test of war. A number of Western states, including Britain, have suggested that, if the use of certain weapons is to be banned, the prohibition should be based on unambiguous scientific evidence that the weapons are 'excessively injurious'. They have also argued that all major states should adhere to the agreement and that the weapons should not be banned if they would then be replaced by equipment having even worse effects. None of these criteria seems entirely satisfactory. The difficulty of obtaining scientific evidence has already been referred to and few states have the technical ability to produce it. The Swedes held a number of demonstrations in the 1970s which were designed to show that small-calibre high-velocity bullets are more destructive than weapons of a larger calibre, because the smaller bullets tend to turn over or 'tumble' in the air and to break up when they enter the human body. However, this was very difficult to prove or disprove. At one demonstration where anaesthetised pigs were shot, the area of wounded flesh removed was determined by the methods used by a particular surgeon rather than by the type of bullet employed.

Yet it should be easier to obtain unambiguous scientific evidence of the relative 'inhumanity' of various rifle bullets than of any of the other weapons which were discussed as candidates for prohibition. In other cases, such as napalm, weapons have to be compared with totally different types of equipment like high explosive to see whether they are more inhumane. Statistics could be compiled to show whether the proportion of deaths amongst those wounded in recent wars by cluster bombs, high explosives or incendiaries has been greater. But it is not clear that the statistics would be very revealing because all sorts of factors, such as the nature of the target — troops in armoured vehicles, or in the open, ammunition dumps or aircraft — could crucially influence casualty figures. Some of those opposed to incendiaries have argued that they produce particularly painful wounds but this would be difficult to quantify. Conversely, the claims of such Western states that, if napalm were banned, the high explosive needed to perform the same function would cause more casualties, would be equally difficult to prove. The fact is that attitudes towards weapons are impressionistic; the employment of poisonous gas was banned by the Geneva Protocol, because people found the use of this weapon unfair or unsavoury, not because it caused excessive fatalities — quite the contrary.

The criterion that all major military states should adhere to an agreement seems no more satisfactory. There is no accepted definition of a major military state. Most of the Third World countries would deny that this label applied to themselves, yet India has a million men under arms and others, such as Saudi Arabia, have some of the most advanced weaponry in the world. Moreover, since most wars now take place inside the communist bloc or in the Third World, it is perhaps more important that Third World states should adhere to an agreement than that the developed states should. The criterion would moreover have ruled out acceptance of the Geneva Protocol until 1975 when the USA decided to ratify it.

Because of the failure of the 'prohibitionist' states to prove that napalm, cluster bombs or high-velocity low-calibre bullets were inhumane, the 1979 conference which was convened to negotiate treaties restricting the use of 'inhumane' weapons, did not prohibit the use of these particular weapons. Agreement was, however, reached on a Dutch-Australian proposal to limit the use of incendiaries, including napalm, in urban areas in order to give some protection to civilians. There was also accord on restricting the use of weapons which contained fragments that could not be detected by X-rays once they entered the body and on a British proposal that minefields should be marked and records made of their location.[14] Again the intention behind this proposal was to protect civilians after the end of the fighting. According to official Polish statistics, 3,834 people (mostly children) were killed in Poland between 1945 and 1975 by weapons left behind after the Second World War and 8,384 were wounded.[15] The war between Britain and Argentina in the spring of 1982 showed just how great the postwar problem caused by modern mines would be. Long after they had ceased to serve any military purpose, Argentine mines continued to pose a really serious threat to those living on the Falklands and their removal was made far more difficult because they could not be detected by metal detectors.

Apart from the Ad Hoc Committee's efforts to limit the use of weaponry in warfare, two parallel efforts were made at the same time. The first of these resulted in the negotiation of a treaty banning the use of Environmental Modification Techniques in warfare (the so-called ENMOD Convention). During the process of negotiation the scope of the treaty's application was gradually narrowed. Parties to the Convention undertake 'not to engage in military or any other hostile use of environmental modification techniques having widespread, long-lasting or severe effects.'[16] Those who wanted to widen the scope of the agreement hoped that it would prohibit the techniques for jungle clearing used by the USA in Vietnam. In the event, however, it would seem only to cover such activities as causing earthquakes under enemy territories and turning tidal waves and tornadoes in their direction. None of these activities is likely to be technically feasible over the next decades but the Convention may become more important as man gains more control over his natural environment.

A more important effort to protect the natural environment and the civilian population was made by the Diplomatic Conference on Humanitarian Law itself. This attempted to modernise the laws of war in the light of the Vietnamese War and other contemporary conflicts. These showed that, although weapons may not have caused a greater proportion of casualties amongst combatants, the civilian population was increasingly at risk. The ideological warfare prevalent in the twentieth century and particularly the prevalence of guerrilla and civil wars meant that the distinction between combatants and non-combatants was becoming ever narrower. The new laws of wars devised by the Conference in October 1980 were based on the premises that 'in any armed conflict the right of the parties to the conflict to choose methods or means of warfare is not unlimited [and] it is prohibited to employ weapons, projectiles and material and methods of warfare of a nature to cause superfluous injury or unnecessary suffering'.[17]

Not only do the new laws of war attempt to protect civilians and combatants but they also prohibit means of warfare causing 'widespread, long-term and severe damage to the natural environment'. Articles in the new agreement prohibited perfidious attempts to kill an enemy under a flag of truce, the use of enemy flags or orders that no quarter should be given to the enemy. The Third World countries inserted clauses in the agreement giving some combatant status to guerrillas and denying the protection of combatant status to mercenaries or to those who are 'motivated to take part in hostilities essentially by the desire for private gain'.

Because of the suffering which recent wars in Vietnam and elsewhere had caused to civilians, the new Geneva code tried to limit the military actions which could be taken against heavily populated areas. Parties to conflicts were obliged to 'direct their operations only against military objectives', and to refrain from 'acts or threats of violence the primary purpose of which is to spread terror among the civilian population'. To prevent indiscriminate shelling and bombing of urban areas, bombardments were prohibited if they treated 'as a single military object a number of clearly separated and distinct military objectives located in a city, town, village or other area . . . ' Furthermore, armies were forbidden to starve enemy peoples by destroying their crops or dams unless these were being specifically used by enemy forces.

The new regulations are undoubtedly a brave attempt to reduce the destruction and deaths caused by warfare. They apply only to conventional and guerrilla conflicts – at least in the eyes of the Western NWS. The US representative stated on 9 June 1977, 'from the outset of the Conference, it has been our understanding that the rules to be developed have been designed with a view to conventional weapons.'[18] He did not mention chemical and biological weapons but went on to argue that 'nuclear weapons are the subject of separate negotiations and agreements'. Thus, he carefully preserved the element of deterrence which nuclear weapons produce. Whilst some have argued that this is a major weakness, in practice the main problem is the complexity of the new rules and the difficulty of abiding by them in actual wars. Since the agreement was reached, whole cities have been destroyed in warfare in Iran and the Lebanon and the population has undoubtedly suffered terrible casualties. In the heat of combat all sorts of regulations may break down. For example, part of a force may decide to surrender whilst another part keeps fighting. This may have been what happened in the battle for Goose Green during the Falklands War in 1982. Some Argentine soldiers surrendered but when British servicemen advanced they were shot down. Such actions probably increase rather than reduce the ferocity of warfare.

A survey of past agreements and current governmental expectations underlies the fragility of attempts to limit warfare once it has begun. If they are only minimal agreements, such as the ENMOD Convention, they may survive but they will have done little to make warfare less destructive. On the other hand, if they would have a substantial impact, the pressure to breach them in wartime will be intense. After the Anglo-German naval agreement of 1935, the Germans agreed that 'from now on [they] will abstain in any future war from the unrestricted use of the submarine for blockade purposes'.[19] Subsequently Aneurin Bevan asked whether it was likely 'if a nation [was] on the verge of defeat and victory [could] be obtained by violating that Convention it [would] stick to it'. Bevan was hardly a grim realist in foreign affairs but he did not want to put too much weight on agreements and Germany was in fact to breach the agreements limiting submarine attacks on merchant ships long before it reached the situation described by Bevan. Bevan's views were similar to those put forward by a French delegate at Geneva during conversations in 1932 about the possibility of limiting bombing attacks. The delegate argued: 'a general fighting in defence of his country was bound to use every means in his power to resist aggression, and could not be denied the use of so effective a weapon'.[20]

It is perfectly clear that states behave in wartime in ways that they would consider outrageous in peacetime. One has only to cite the examples of the Allied take-overs of Iran[21] and Iceland during the Second World War to prove the point. It is also clear that belligerents can usually find excuses for breaking agreements if they wish to do so. On 17 April 1915 German wireless communiqués claimed falsely that the British had used gas shells east of Ypres. Five days later the Germans used gas themselves. A British official commented 17 years later: 'this is a precedent that might well be followed by an enemy desiring to cloak a breach of the convention under the plea of retaliation'.[22] A more bizarre incident took place in 1933 when the German government claimed that an air attack had been made against Berlin. It used this as an argument for the need for German rearmament. Two years later the Italians accused the Abyssinians of torturing and killing prisoners, killing civilians and using expanding bullets to justify the use of poisonous gas in 1935 and 1936.[23] Whether or not the Abyssinians behaved in the way alleged by the Italians is beside the point, they had no way of deterring the use of chemical weapons. In future wars any of the agreements limiting the methods of fighting could be breached if the belligerents had enough incentive to do so. It may be that nations treat prisoners of war well because they hope that their own servicemen will be well treated if they are held captive. Consequently nations which are indifferent to the wellbeing of their own peoples also mistreat their enemies if it is militarily convenient to do so.

Critics of non-use agreements sometimes argue that we should not try to make conventional war more humane because this would encourage states to fight. But it is fair to say that agreements would have to be far more wide-ranging than any so far attempted before the attractiveness of conventional war was substantially increased. Most of the developed countries which have experienced general war over the last 70 years have emerged from the experience thoroughly chastened.[24] A more substantial argument is that we should not take a 'luddite' approach to advances in weaponry. As argued earlier, by and large, such advances have decreased the destructiveness of warfare.[25] Contemporary improvements in the accuracy of weapons may make it possible to destroy bridges and other military targets without devastating the surrounding countryside. We have to beware that agreements do not check such advances.

Conclusion

Non-use agreements are of most importance to the Third World because this is where the majority of wars have taken place since 1945. In conflicts within the Soviet bloc — were reports of Soviet use of chemical and biological weapons in Afghanistan and South East Asia to prove accurate[26] — such agreements would appear to have little impact. As far as the central 'balance' is concerned, there are two dangers in any agreement of this type. Firstly in democracies it often proves difficult to find funds for weapons whose use in war is theoretically forbidden. Thus, the NATO nations have ceased to produce chemical weapons even though they believe that the Russians have very large stocks. Yet in every case where chemical weapons have been used, it has been against states which were not then in a position to retaliate. Hence in a war the West might be faced by mass attacks with chemical weapons against which it had no means of retaliation except the use of nuclear weapons.

The second danger is that non-use agreements might spread into the nuclear area and undermine deterrence. As we shall see, there has long been pressure for agreements to ban the use of nuclear weapons. The danger in any such agreement is that it might marginally reduce the fear of nuclear war and encourage states to take greater risks. On the other hand, it is unlikely that an agreement of this sort would actually effect the decision to use nuclear weapons in the desperate situation where such use appeared possible. The primary object of all arms control must continue to be to reduce the likelihood of war. Humanising warfare may be a secondary aim but when the two clash it is clear which should have priority.

Notes

1. Letter from Air Vice Marshal Menaul in *The Times*, 2 August 1977.
2. *Arms Control; A Survey and Appraisal of Multilateral Agreements*, SIPRI, 1978 (hereafter referred to as *Arms Control*), p. 55 passim, Article 25.
3. Loc. cit., pp. 53 and 54.
4. Ulrich Trumpener, 'the road to Ypres, the beginnings of gas warfare in World War I', *Journal of Modern History*, September 1975.
5. L.F. Haber, 'gas warfare, the legend and the facts', the Stevenson lecture, 25 November 1975, Bedford College, London.
6. SIPRI, *The Problem of Chemical and Biological Warfare*, Vol. 1, Humanities Press, New York, 1971, p. 143.
7. *Documents on Disarmament 1945-59*, Vol. 1, p. 377.
8. S. Kozlov, 'progress on banning chemical weapons can give impetus to disarmament', *Soviet News*, 7 August 1979. For British preparations in Second World War, see J. Lewis, 'Churchill and the "Anthrax bomb" ', *Encounter*, February 1982.
9. Asbjorn Eide, 'outlawing the use of certain conventional weapons, another approach to disarmament?' International Peace Research Institute, Oslo.
10. R.R. Baxter, 'conventional weapons under legal prohibitions', *International Security*, winter 1977.
11. FO/83/1695, see particularly the letter from Dr Ogston of the Department of Surgery at the University of Aberdeen, 2 May 1899.
12. FO/83/1702, War Office to the Foreign Office, 17 May 1899.
13. Lt Colonel R. Scott, 'battlefield injury the scope for surgery', *Journal of the Royal Army Medical Corps*, 1976.
14. 'Rules to cover new kinds of conflict', *The Times*, 8 May 1978; 'UN conference urges curb on incendiary weapons', loc. cit., 10 October 1980.
15. Working paper on certain conventional weapons which may be deemed to be excessively injurious or to have indiscriminate effects', Ministry of Foreign Affairs, Stockholm, June 1978, p. 28.
16. *Arms Control*, p. 123, Article 1.
17. *Arms Control*, p. 126, section 1, Article 35.
18. *Documents on Disarmament 1977*, pp. 359-60.
19. ADM/116/3377. See also S.W. Roskill, *Naval Policy between the Wars*, Vol 2, Collins, London, 1976, p. 304 passim.
20. Memorandum of 6 July 1932, ADM/116/3618.
21. Claremont Skrine, *World War in Iran*, Constable, London, 1962, p. 74 passim.

22. Minute by the Secretary of the Committee of Imperial Defence, 25 November 1932, ADM/116/3618.
23. See Note 6 supra.
24. P. Towle, 'the decline of the English warrior', *Quadrant*, September 1980.
25. Some figures for casualties are contained in F. Beer, *Peace against War*, W.H. Freeman, San Francisco, 1981, p. 34 passim. See also G. Elliot, *Twentieth Century Book of the Dead*, Allen Lane, Penguin Press, 1972.
26. See Chapter 11 below.

5 THE PRAGMATIC APPROACH

Arms control agreements should not struggle against the strategic 'tide' but should reinforce those 'tides' which make for peace. Nowhere is this more so than in the Great Powers' relationships with the Third World. It is not the arms race which threatens world peace but the possibility that the Great Powers might become involved in a direct confrontation because of their role in one of the numerous wars in the Third World. Fortunately, over the last century all sorts of methods have been developed by pragmatic statesmen for fighting 'by proxy', rather than involving their countries directly. It is these methods which arms control should strengthen, not oppose.

There is a spectrum of ways in which the Great Powers can aid friendly states, running from trade and economic aid on the one side through the supply of arms and advisers to the sending of armed forces thinly disguised as 'volunteers' on the other side of the spectrum. Some say that such aid leads inevitably to involvement by the donor, others argue that it turns the proxy into the 'cat's paw' of the Great Power. Neither criticism is valid, as the history of the last 100 years demonstrates.

Arms Transfers

As weapons became more complex in the nineteenth century, so the transfer of large quantities of armaments from neutrals to belligerents increasingly influenced the outcome of wars. The growing complexity of weapons made it difficult for even the most powerful and advanced countries to produce all the weapons they wanted during a war. The issue produced great controversy during the American Civil War because of the scale of Confederate purchases in England and elsewhere; 'the Confederate Army, contrary to tradition, was practically supplied after 1861 . . . by the importation of small arms from abroad'.[1] Even more controversial than supplies to the Southern army was the question of the purchase of warships by the Southern states in Britain. In the end, Britain bowed to pressure from Washington and prevented vessels leaving the yards where they were being built to fight for the Confederate navy.[2] However, the sale of armaments went on, though not without protests. Britain was not drawn into the war on the Confederate side, nor, if the Southerners had established their independence, would they have become Britain's cat's paw.

In the next major war, the Franco-Prussian War of 1870, historians have described how,

French agents scoured the markets of the world for arms and ammunition. French naval supremacy gave unrestricted access to the arsenals of Great Britain and the United States, where manufacturers gratefully seized the opportunity to unload stocks of obsolescent rifles and to experiment with new models. In spite of official protests from Berlin and mounting rage in Germany, armaments and military equipment were freely imported across the Channel and the Atlantic.[3]

Again the suppliers were not drawn into the war, nor was there any feeling that the French were acting as their proxy. There may have been widespread sympathy for France's predicament but there was little attempt to do anything directly to help France but offer to mediate.

In the First World War the outcome was different. Access to overseas supplies of armaments was as important as it had been in the American Civil and Franco-Prussian Wars. A month after the war had begun, the German ambassador in Washington was warning his government that French missions had begun to visit the Bethlehem steel works in search of munitions.[4] Congressmen from the Middle West protested against the supply of armaments to the Allies and by December 1914 Congress was flooded with appeals against the trade. Consequently Allied representatives in Washington began to exert pressure on President Wilson to resist these attacks on US arms supplies, actual and potential.[5] President Wilson himself seems to have had doubts about the desirability of the sale of armaments. Yet, historians critical of his policies have argued, 'the Administration desired to see the Allies win and declined to take any action even in defense of American neutral rights which would seriously interfere with that objective'.[6] Certainly, Secretary of State Bryan resigned because he considered Wilson insufficiently neutral and he was replaced by Lansing who was more sympathetic to the Allied cause. Lansing pointed out that the sale of armaments to belligerents was perfectly legal and that, if their sale were halted, this would. only encourage states to build up their armaments in peacetime.[7]

After the end of the war there was a strong feeling in the United

States that the country had declared war in 1917 because of its arms sales policy. According to Walter Millis's influential book, *Road to War, America 1914-1917*, 'when a great munitions industry had been organised in the United States and the allies were dependent upon it, it was too late.' Because of this development 'our neutrality was at an end. After that our actual military participation was largely a question of chance'.[8] But this analysis was wholly inadequate. Many in the United States, including the President and Lansing, sympathised with the Allies more than they did with the Central Powers. As a result they probably hoped that US arms sales would allow Britain, France and Russia to win the war. But it was doubts about this outcome, together with anger over German submarine policy and meddling in Mexico, which precipitated the US declaration of war.

Conversely, Britain and France did not become the United States cat's paw because of the financial and military support which they received from Washington. In the first months of the Paris peace conference, President Wilson wielded a good deal of influence, partly because of his popularity in Europe, partly because of US power, and partly because of gratitude for the help given after the USA became directly involved inthe fighting. But, at no stage were Georges Clemenceau and Lloyd George, the French and British leaders, easily influenced by the United States, as Wilson would ruefully have attested. Because of the widespread misunderstandings in the United States about the reasons for the country's decision to declare war in 1917, Congress passed a series of Acts in the 1930s designed to prevent it again becoming embroiled in a war by the sale of armaments. Consequently when the Second World War broke out, 'no supply of arms or munitions [to belligerents] was possible at all until the repeal of the arms embargo by the revised Neutrality Act of 4 November 1939'.[9]

Despite their stand in the First World War, British leaders also continued to have a feeling that the supply of armaments to belligerents was unneutral and was likely to lead to involvement in a war, as their behaviour showed during the Spanish Civil War. The Conservative renegade, Winston Churchill, claimed that he was for 'rigid neutrality' in that case and therefore against the sale of armaments to the belligerents.[10] The Foreign Secretary, Anthony Eden, told the Spanish ambassador in London that he would consider licensing the sale of weapons. But he very soon changed his mind, despite the fact that the ambassador represented a legitimate government and that there was no legal need to be neutral in a war between government and rebel forces.[11] Similarly, in the United States, President Roosevelt's Act against the supply of arms to Spain passed the Senate by 81 to none and the House by 406 to one.[12] However, when the Second World War began, Roosevelt quickly found ways of helping the Allies.

The period from September 1939 to December 1941 laid to rest for many years the prevalent idea that the supply of armaments to belligerents would lead automatically to involvement in a war. However unneutral the United States' behaviour became in this period, Hitler had sufficient interest in keeping the Americans out of the war to avoid confronting them head on. He was hardly in a position to complain about their actions as he was a master of the art of vicarious belligerency himself.

Since the Second World War, the supply of armaments to belligerents and to states on the verge of belligerency has become a major facet of the strategy of the Great Powers. Arms transfers have also become an important way in which one Great Power can signal to another the significance which it attaches to the outcome of a local conflict or a possible future one – as the United States showed in 1980 by announcing its intention of supplying arms to Pakistan to try to prevent the Soviet-Afghan conflict spreading into Pakistani territory. Arms transfers enabled the United States to support Israel and the Soviet Union to arm the Arab states without becoming involved in the Middle East wars themselves. Were this not possible, they would often have been faced with the alternatives of seeing friendly states defeated or of actually sending ground forces to participate in the successive conflicts. Moreover, it seems likely that arms supplies will be even more important in future wars because of the speed at which munitions are used up and destroyed.

Arms transfers to other countries are once again frequently criticised by Western liberals who argue that they encourage the outbreak of wars and intensify the fighting should war break out. But we have already seen that arms races are not the cause of war as some suppose. Furthermore, as we have also seen, it is incorrect to say that more advanced weapons cause more destruction. As a general rule, the more advanced the weapon, the less likely it is to be used, or used effectively in Third World combats. In the Iran-Iraq War which began in September 1980, it was small arms and artillery which caused the damage and dominated the fighting, whilst the advanced F14s possessed by the Iranians played little part in the conflict.

Politically, the effort to curb arms sales to the Third World countries is intensely resented amongst the developing states themselves. They argue, as the Syrian representative once claimed at the United Nations, 'their defence was their own concern and their sovereign right'.[13] What is strategically more important is that liberals often overlook the part which arms transfers have played in distancing the Great Powers from conflicts in various parts of the world. Of course, some might argue that Great Powers should not interfere at all but, since such interference is likely to continue, it is the task of the strategist to ensure that it is carried out with the minimum risk of general war.

In recent years liberals have revived Walter Millis's claim that arms transfers draw states into unwanted wars. When the USA was supplying arms on a great scale to the Shah's government in Iran, some commentators argued that the presence of large numbers of American instructors and engineers in Iran meant that the United States might be involved in any conflict in which Iran itself was embroiled. In fact British troops were located in the Indian subcontinent in 1947 without Britain taking part in the first Indo-Pakistan War; Soviet advisers were present in North Vietnam during the Vietnam War and in the Middle East during the Arab-Israeli War, yet the Soviet Union did not itself become involved in these conflicts. Arms sales can be a surrogate for direct Great Power involvement in a local conflict, rather than the cause of such involvement. If a friendly state is defeated, despite the arms with which a Great Power has supplied it, the Great Power can decide to intervene with its own forces. However, it is not the supply of armaments which is the cause of this involvement but the failure of such supplies to achieve the Great Power's purposes.

Volunteers

If the supply of armaments fails, the Great Power can turn to the provision of 'volunteers' to help friendly states. This practice became widespread between the two world wars and particularly during the Spanish Civil War and the fighting in China. Mercenary armies are, of course, as old as written history itself and they have played a very significant part in Europe's wars. Similarly volunteers in large numbers fought on the French side in the Franco-Prussian War.[14] Germans, French and even Russians also fought on the Boer side against the British in 1899 and the Boer 'Staatsartillery' was almost exclusively recruited in Holland. But these were genuine volunteers; Hitler, Stalin and Mussolini instituted the practice of sending military units to a foreign campaign in the guise of volunteers. Many of the traditional diplomats and statesmen reacted to this new practice with predictable distaste. Anthony

Eden complained to a Welsh audience in October 1937,

> obligations are ignored, engagements cynically torn up, confidence
> has been shaken, methods of making war without declaring war are
> being adopted, while all the time each nation declares that its one
> desire is peace.[15]

The German Foreign Ministry was no more enthusiastic than the British
either about the practice of selling arms to combatants in Spain or
about the decision to send 'volunteers'.[16] Yet the 'volunteers' were a
brilliant and original idea. They enabled Germany, Russia and Italy to
test their weapons, to train their men in combat and, most importantly,
to support 'their side' in the war without too much risk to themselves.
There was no contradiction between such a policy and their professed
desire for peace. On the contrary, the policy was designed to guard the
advantages of a general peace, whilst achieving some of the benefits of
fighting a limited war.

A 'Tourist Group' of Germans for Spain was established in the
middle of 1936 and the first group of 'volunteers' left Hamburg for
Cadiz at the end of July.[17] For the next two years, four transport aircraft carrying men and supplies left Germany for Spain each week and a
cargo boat departed for the same destination on average once every five
days. Soviet practice was similar. One historian of the Civil War has
speculated that Stalin had the idea of sending volunteers to fight on the
Republican side because Czech, German and Italian prisoners of war
had fought in the Russian Civil War.[18] Whether Stalin was influenced by
this experience or not, the Russian leader indulged in the new policy as
enthusiastically as his Italian and German counterparts. There were large
numbers of genuine volunteers going to Spain, particularly on the
Republican side, and this helped the totalitarian states to maintain the
transparent pretence that their own forces came into this category.
When Hitler met Neville Chamberlain in Munich in September 1938, he
told the British Prime Minister, 'he would be delighted to withdraw the
few German volunteers who were there, as soon as ever the others were
willing to do the same'.[19] How one could so easily withdraw a genuine
volunteer was not explained and Chamberlain was sufficiently cowed to
avoid pointing out the contradiction in terms.

While the Italians, Russians and Germans were developing and
exploring the limits of their new strategy in Spain, similar events were
unfolding on the other side of the world. 'During the decades between
the wars almost every Chinese war lord of consequence boasted a few

foreign-made airplanes and some foreign pilots to fly them against his foes'.[20] Such foreign pilots were genuine soldiers of fortune but a new development took place in 1934 when Mussolini sent an official mission of 40 military pilots, headed by General Scaroni, to help the Chinese Nationalists. Again this development was in part the result of the growing complexity of military science. They were sent in the belief that a small number of advisers could make a difference to the outcome of the war, depending on the calibre of the advisers or, more importantly, the potential of those they were advising. General Holman and others had failed to stiffen the Whites in the Russian Civil War sufficiently to enable them to defeat the Communists. Moreover, the experience probably did little to recommend this method of aiding parties in a civil war to British politicians. On the other hand, French advisers under General Weygand may, for a time, have helped the Poles defeat the Russians in 1920.[21]

General Scaroni and his men appear to have had little impact on events in China. The leading US volunteer in China in the 1930s, Major General Chennault, came to believe that the Italians were actually sabotaging the Chinese war effort and they were withdrawn when the fighting against Japan intensified. The American government also tried to persuade all the US nationals helping the Chinese to return home. Fortunately for the Chinese Chennault and others disobeyed their government and,

> while American diplomats were busy prodding American airmen out of China, the Red Air Force arrived. The Russians sent four fighter and two bomber squadrons completely staffed and equipped to fight the Japs in China [in 1937].[22]

The government in Moscow was so impervious to Japanese resentment against the aid which it was giving to China that Tokyo did not even consider it worthwhile protesting. Stalin seems to have decided that the Japanese understood nothing but military strength and, when the two countries' forces clashed on the frontier, Soviet armies inflicted a crushing defeat on the Japanese.[23] However, in 1939 Soviet advisers were withdrawn from China, presumably because of the deterioration in the world situation. The Japanese were then free to use their Zero fighters and their bombers to terrorise the Chinese into submission. The Chinese sent Chennault to Washington to beg for modern US aircraft and for trained US pilots to fight them. Even after the experience in Spain and China, democratic politicians and officials were unwilling to copy the dictators' methods. With some reluctance the Chinese were sold 100 P40 fighters but Chennault's request for officers to fly them was turned down. Chennault pointed out that the German, Italian and Russian governments had employed their men in combat without becoming directly involved themselves but his pleas were ignored. Even in April 1941 it took 'direct personal intervention from President Roosevelt to pry the pilots and ground crews from the army and navy'.[24]

During the Second World War there were many examples from Yugoslavia to Laos and from Malaya to France of Allied military missions being sent to help anti-Axis insurgents. Subsequently, democratic statesmen have been less reluctant to emulate the dictators and to employ pseudo-volunteers. The Great Powers have increasingly sent official advisers and volunteers to bolster the government of the newly independent nations, or unofficial help to the guerrillas who are fighting to overthrow them. There is the usual spectrum of such aid from financial assistance, through arms supplies and the attachment of advisers to the employment of pseudo-volunteers in combat and finally to the formal commitment of ground troops. Usually help is confined to financial aid and arms transfers but, in the most dramatic case — Vietnam — the United States eventually moved through the whole spectrum of assistance. 'American involvement in Southeast Asia was so gradual as to be almost casual, a slowly escalating process all but defying determination of a precise starting point'.[25]

The USA financed French efforts to defeat the Vietminh until 1954. Then, when the French were ejected and the country was divided by the Geneva agreement, the USA began to aid the non-communist Southern government under Ngo dinh Diem. By 1956, Diem was receiving 250 million dollars in aid, and US supplies and advisers were helping to strengthen his army. In the early 1960s President Kennedy allowed these advisers to go into battle with their South Vietnamese colleagues. It was not, however, until after Kennedy's assassination that President Johnson began in 1965 to send complete military units to fight against the Vietcong.

The ultimate failure of US policies in Indochina by no means suggests that all efforts of this sort are doomed to such a fate, although it does indicate where the dangers lie. US prestige became so bound up with South Vietnam that, at each stage in the conflict's progress, the US government preferred to increase its involvement rather than to abandon Indochina completely. But the administrations had plenty of occasions when they could have reversed the drift to war. There was nothing inevitable about the process. Moreover, even though it was totally dependent upon US support, the South Vietnamese government never became amenable to all US demands. At every period it was clear that, if it defeated the Vietcong, it would follow its own course in world affairs.

Other Great Powers have preferred to see their clients defeated rather than to put in their own troops. Thus, the Kremlin has watched the successive defeats of the Arabs without embroiling its own forces. Presumably this was because they wanted to mobilise overwhelming forces before they intervened and because of a fear of involving the USA on the other side — a fear which was certainly encouraged by US signals during the 1973 Arab-Israeli War. In areas close to their own frontiers — Hungary, Czechoslovakia and Afghanistan — the Russians have been less reluctant to commit their own forces, although their behaviour over Poland in 1981 shows that, even there, they would prefer to keep control by non-military means.

Genuine volunteers still exist in the modern world and give some 'cover' to the activities of the Great Powers. Jews from the United States and other Western countries volunteered to help the Israelis in recent Middle Eastern wars out of national or religious sympathy, while Iranians and other Moslems have volunteered to fight for the Palestinians. White soldiers of fortune have fought in the Congo and in the Nigerian civil wars. They also volunteered to join the Rhodesian armed forces out of political sympathy, the desire to participate in combat and perhaps to earn the wages offered. Sometimes genuine volunteers and official advisers have been mixed together. After 1970 the Sultan of Oman's forces were expanded to fight the guerrillas operating inside the country. The Sultan was helped by the United Kingdom which 'also assisted to the extent of seconding officers and men of all three Services to fill key positions in the Sultan's Armed Forces. In addition, several hundred ex-service personnel contracted to serve the Sultan filling positions for which Omanis were as yet untrained'.[26]

In recent years, the communists have further refined the strategy of vicarious belligerency. The Russians have supported Cuban intervention in Angola and Ethiopia, thus bringing up to date the measures employed by the dictatorships during the Spanish Civil War. Unlike the Italians, Germans and Russians in Spain, the Cubans are openly and officially sent by their government, but the Cuban government can take risks of this sort precisely because Cuba is not a Great Power. The French have also used regular Moroccan troops to help support the pro-Western government in Zaire, but this incident was on a smaller scale and shorter-lived than the Soviet-Cuban effort. According to some calculations, up to 50,000 Cuban troops are now engaged in training and military operations in Africa, forming a long-range striking force of considerable military and political value. The Cubans can undertake operations which would provoke outrage if they were carried out by a Great (White) Power. Moreover, the Russians benefit because, if their Cuban allies are defeated, their own prestige is not at stake. When Mussolini's troops were defeated by the Spanish Republicans at Guadaljara, he vowed that none of them would return alive to Italy until they had secured a victory.[27] Thus he greatly increased the intensity of the Italian commitment to Franco's forces. Similarly, direct Soviet intervention in Afghanistan in 1980 meant that the Kremlin's prestige was at stake in a way that it was not hazarded by the activities of the Cubans in Africa.

The criticisms by Mr Brzezinski, Dr Kissinger and others of Soviet and Cuban activities in Africa closely resemble Eden's criticisms of the behaviour of the dictatorships during the Spanish Civil War.[28] Such outrage is perfectly satisfactory so long as it is seen as part of the game, part of the effort to convince public opinion that the Russians are behaving in unacceptable ways. But the correct response to Cuban activities was to aid their opponents, not to jettison detente. In the long run the West may have to find its own equivalents to the Cubans if it wants to compete successfully in the Third World.

The Role of Arms Control

If the United States administration abandoned the effort to persuade Congress to ratify SALT II in order to persuade the Russians to withdraw from Afghanistan, then it was grossly exaggerating the importance of the arms control lever and the significance which the Kremlin ascribed to SALT. If, on the other hand, it was merely trying to 'punish' the Soviet leaders then it was under a misapprehension that arms control agreements were a favour that the USA granted the USSR rather than a bargain in which both sides made some losses and some gains. Nevertheless, one should recognise that Soviet intervention in Afghanistan was more undesirable than Cuban activities in Africa, precisely because the armies of a Super Power were directly involved. The question is whether any agreement between the USA and the USSR could make a repetition of this sort of direct intervention less likely.

It is just conceivable that, at some stage, the Russians might welcome such an agreement. The war against the Moslem guerrillas in Afghanistan has tied down up to one hundred thousand Soviet troops and somewhat tarnished the Soviet image in the Third World. Conversely, Soviet experience with the use of Cubans in Ethiopia and Angola has been much more rewarding. If the Cubans had been defeated, the Kremlin could have washed its hands of them. But, since they have been militarily quite successful, it can bask in their reflected glory. Seeing the advantages of such indirect intervention and the disadvantages of their direct action in Afghanistan, Soviet leaders might be prepared to come to some sort of agreement placing limits on direct Super Power involvement in the developing countries. The problem is to find an acceptable and meaningful distinction between 'legitimate' and 'illegitimate' actions, given that spheres of influence are no longer possible.

The Western powers would also have to make up their minds what sort of agreement they want. On the one side a very restrictive agreement would preclude almost all direct military intervention in the Third World. The British government has, for example, agreed to give direct military assistance to Belize after it became independent in September 1981 in order to protect it from Guatemala which has claims on its territory. A very restrictive agreement would preclude this sort of intervention which interferes in Belize-Guatemalan relations. On the other hand, if the agreement simply prevented intervention when such an action was not demanded by the government of the small power, it is very difficult to see what it would achieve. This would permit the sorts of 'military assistance' to Afghanistan and Ethiopia against which Western governments have protested, since the Russians would argue that the Afghan and Ethiopian governments have asked for help.

In the Afghan case this defence is clearly bogus since the Afghan government did not ask for help. It was overthrown and its leader killed after Soviet intervention.[29] To prevent this sort of take-over, the United States and the Soviet Union might agree that they would not send combat troops into a non-aligned country until the government of that country had registered a request for such troops either with the UN, or with the Bureau of Non Aligned Nations in New Delhi or with some regional organisation such as the Organisation of African Unity. The first obstacle to such a suggestion is that it is sometimes necessary for a Great Power to act rapidly. Thus the British felt that they had to land troops very quickly in Kuwait in 1961 in order to forestall what the Kuwaiti government believed was a threatened invasion from Iraq. The second main obstacle might well be the opposition of Third World governments to an agreement which limited their sovereignty and the embarrassment they would feel in any admission that they had asked a Great Power for military help. The first obstacle could perhaps be overcome but nothing except the willingness of the Third World countries themselves to accept the scheme could overcome the second. The Super Powers and the other European nations have already agreed in the Final Act of the CSCE that they will

refrain in their mutual relations, as well as in their international relations in general, from the threat or use of force against the territorial integrity or political independence of any state or in any other manner inconsistent with the purposes of the United Nations and the present Declaration. No consideration can be invoked to warrant resort to the threat or use of force in contravention of this principle.

It was because of the insertion of this principle into the Final Act that the European countries felt able to bring up the question of Afghanistan at the Madrid CSCE review and to accuse the Soviet Union of being in breach of the agreement. It would seem worthwhile to reiterate a principle of this sort in any agreement between the Super Powers on relations with the Third World.

A much more 'mechanical' sort of agreement would restrict the total number of combat troops which a Super Power could maintain in the territory of a non-aligned state. For the West this would present problems because of US military bases in Cuba and perhaps elsewhere. Moreover the limit would have to be set high enough to permit assistance of the type supplied by Britain to Belize but not high enough to make it easy for the Great Power to repress the majority of the population of a Third World country. Nevertheless, such an agreement might encourage the use of proxy war techniques. Serving officers might be replaced in military missions to Third World countries by those on the retired list. Logistic support could be provided by civilian engineering and contracting firms.

The three measures outlined above — registration of requests from Third World countries for military assistance from the Great Powers; reaffirmation of the principles enshrined in the Final Act; and some numerical total on the number of troops which the Great Powers could maintain in the territory of a non-aligned state — should be regarded as akin to the European CBMs. They could hardly lay claim to solve the problems involved in relations between the Great Powers and the Third World. But they might make it marginally less likely that there would be bitter controversies of the type which have broken out between the Soviet Union and the West in recent years and encourage the development of war by proxy rather than direct intervention.

Notes

1. K.F.C. Owsley, *King Cotton Diplomacy*, University of Chicago Press, 1959, p. 266. See also E.D. Adams, *Great Britain and the American Civil War*, Russell and Russell, New York, undated, p. 116.
2. Owsley, *King Cotton Diplomacy*, pp. 403-8.
3. M. Howard, *The Franco-Prussian War, The German Invasion of France*, Rupert Hart-Davis, London, 1962, p. 246.
4. Walter Millis, *Road to War, America 1914-1917*, Howard Fertig, New York, 1970, p. 98.
5. Ibid., pp. 99-100.
6. E. Borchard and W.P. Lage, *Neutrality for the United States*, Yale University Press, New Haven, 1940, p. 34.
7. *War Memoirs of Robert Lansing*, Bobbs Merrill, New York, 1935, p. 56.
8. Millis, *Road to War*, pp. 101-2 and 221.
9. H. Duncan Hall, *History of the Second World War, North Atlantic Supply*, HMSO, London, 1955, p. 41.
10. Hugh Thomas, *The Spanish Civil War*, Hamish Hamilton, London, 1977, p. 344 passim.
11. *The Eden Memoirs, Facing the Dictators*, Cassell, London, 1962, pp. 400 and 415.
12. Thomas, *Spanish Civil War*, p. 573 passim.
13. 805 Meeting of the U.N. First Committee, 7 December 1955.
14. Howard, *Franco-Prussian War*, p. 252.
15. Eden, *Memoirs*, p. 473.
16. Thomas, *Spanish Civil War*, p. 359. See also *Documents on German Foreign Policy, 1918-1945*, Series D, Volume III, *Germany and the Spanish Civil War*, document number 10, p. 10.
17. Thomas, *Spanish Civil War*, p. 357.
18. Thomas, ibid., pp. 452-3.
19. *Documents on British Foreign Policy, 1919-1939*, Third Series, Vol 2, HMSO, London, 1949, no. 1228, p. 636.
20. Robert Hotz (ed.), *Way of a Fighter, The Memoirs of Claire Lee Chennault*, G.P. Putnam, New York, 1949, p. 36.
21. J.M. Roberts (ed.), *Europe in the 20th Century*, Vol. 2, Macdonald, London, 1971, p. 289 passim.
22. Hotz, *Way of a Fighter*, p. 61.
23. A.D. Cox, 'The Kwantung Army and the Nomonhan Incident', *Military Affairs*, October 1969.
24. Hotz, *Way of a Fighter*, p. 102.
25. D.R. Palmer, *Summons of the Trumpet: US-Vietnam in Perspective*, Presidio, San Rafael, 1978, p. 3.
26. Major General K. Perkins, 'Oman the End of the War', *RUSI Journal*, March 1979.
27. Thomas, *Spanish Civil War*, p. 604.
28. 'Kissinger, priority for nuclear arms problem', *The Times*, 15 January 1976.

29. S. Kardar, 'The Soviet Intervention in Afghanistan of 1979 and its Impact on East-West Relations', unpublished MPhil thesis, University of Cambridge, 1982.

Part Two

DIPLOMACY

6 DICTATORS AND DISARMAMENT

Introduction

In Part One I have selected for examination five of the ways in which men try to control weapons and warfare. The disarmers regard weapons *per se* as the cause of warfare and seek to abolish them under the process known as GCD; the arms control lobby seeks stabilising measures which, very often, means equalising the forces of potential enemies, whilst the 'humanitarians' support attempts to limit the use of weapons and so the destructiveness of warfare. At the CSCE European leaders tried to agree upon some limitations on ideological competition, whilst pragmatic leaders have tried to limit their involvement in local wars.

Almost all these approaches are often based on conceptual weaknesses or muddled thinking. Contrary to the beliefs of many disarmers, armaments and armies are not themselves the basic cause of warfare and, even if we could negotiate an agreement to bring about GCD, warfare and violence would continue. The IRA in Northern Ireland have found stolen civilian explosives quite adequate for killing their victims and ordinary hand drills ideal for maiming and torturing them. Contrary to the beliefs of the arms control lobby, equalising the power of potential enemies does not reduce the likelihood of warfare and, contrary to the beliefs of the humanitarians, advances in weaponry have not increased the ratio of deaths to combatants. Furthermore, those leaders and commentators who argued that the role of the CSCE was to enhance East-West confidence side-stepped the question whether such confidence was justified.

Nevertheless, all five approaches have something to offer to the control of weaponry and warfare in the nuclear age, in so far as they can stabilise relations between states and reduce the unpredictability of international events. Clearly the aim of stabilisation, the aim of arms control in general, can only be achieved in certain circumstances. Pursuing my original analogy, arms control is a weak medicine. If the international disease with which we are faced is terminal, like cancer, then any diplomatic agreements will fail, just as aspirin would be unable to halt the progress of such a disease. Faced with a Hitler bent on expanding his empire such palliatives appear misguided or even comic. But, if

the illness is merely influenza, or if the medicine can be combined with
more potent types, then aspirin may be more effective at controlling
the disease.

What can be achieved in the way of arms control will be determined
today by the attitudes of the three great blocs — the West, the Soviet
Union and the Third World — and above all by the political relationships between East and West. It is to these attitudes and relationships
that we turn in this section.

The Nazi Approach

Largely unrestricted by the pressures of public opinion in their own
countries, dictators can cynically manipulate disarmament conferences
to serve their revisionist ends, to justify their actions and to weaken the
resolution of their potential enemies. Nowhere is this better illustrated
than in Adolf Hitler's policies towards the League of Nation's Conference on the Reduction and Limitation of Armaments which met in
1932. Hitler's democratic predecessors in office had very quickly made
clear that they would not accept any outcome to the Conference which
did not involve recognition of a German 'right' to equality of treatment
with other nations and particularly to military equality with France.[1]
The German delegation argued that France should disarm down to the
German level and, when its demands for equality were not met, it withdrew from the Conference in July 1932. The Germans did not rejoin
the Conference until January 1933, just before Hitler came to power.
But German policy did not appear to change under the new leader. The
German delegation was told that it must continue to work for a 'posi-
tive' outcome, in other words for the acceptance of the idea of Franco-
German military equality. However, the implicit threat that, if Germany's
demands were not met, it would rearm, was much more credible under
Hitler than it had been under his predecessors.

Hitler did not believe that nations would ever disarm by agreement.
He claimed in private that: 'it was obvious that the sole purpose of the
Disarmament Conference was either to break up the Reichswehr or
saddle Germany with the blame for the failure of the Conference.'[2]
Nevertheless, there was little about his attitudes or about German
policy in general which a reasonably cynical observer could not deduce
from German statements at the Conference. Nadolny, the leader of the
Reich's delegation, reported on 3 June 1933 that he had told the Conference,

---

on the basis of the Treaties (Article 8 of the Covenant and the preamble of part V of the Versailles Treaty) and as a member of the League of Nations, Germany has the right to claim that, after she herself has disarmed, the disarmament of the other states should be carried through.[3]

In April 1933 Nadolny had suggested that Germany should demand that a zone inside the French border should be demilitarised equal in area to the Rhineland zone demilitarised by the Treaty of Versailles. He went on to explain that he did not expect his proposal to be accepted but his aim was to work for the remilitarisation of the Rhineland. The German Foreign Minister, Neurath, replied that to introduce such a proposal at this stage of the negotiations would too obviously be destructive.[4] Instead he suggested that Germany should ask for compensation for the demilitarisation of the Rhineland in any agreement on force levels.

As time went on the Germans made less and less effort to hide their intentions should their proposals be, as they expected, rejected. Neurath told the British Foreign Secretary, Sir John Simon, 'we had to insist that we be permitted at once to procure all the arms that were not prohibited to others'.[5] He complained to the French that Germany 'had been robbed by the Treaty of Versailles of all natural rights of a free nation'.[6] Consequently, when the French refused to disarm, Hitler decided in October 1933 to withdraw from the Conference and from the League of Nations. At the same time he kept up his propaganda to reduce the democratic nations' response.

> The German government and the German nation are united in their determination to carry on a policy of peace, conciliation and understanding as a basis of all decisions and actions ... They would gladly agree to any actual disarmament of the world, with the assurance of their readiness to destroy even the last German machine gun and to discharge the last man from the army if other nations decide to do the same.[7]

Sometimes some assurances appear to have lulled the suspicions of Western statesmen. The German ambassador in France reported in February 1934 that, when he had told Anthony Eden that Hitler was a man of peace, 'Eden vigorously agreed with me on this and declared that the English government was absolutely convinced that these were the maxims of the Reich Chancellor ... The attempt must be made to convince the French of this likewise.'[8] But the real purpose of Hitler's public pronouncements was to appeal to the disarmament lobby and to public opinion in the democracies in general. The dictators were only too well aware how important public opinion was. Mussolini told the German ambassador, England 'approached the whole problem [of disarmament] from the point of view of domestic politics'.[9] Hitler and Mussolini had no great need to pay attention to public opinion and it is not clear that their public wanted disarmament or wanted it as much as they wanted the rectification of the 'wrongs' done to them at Versailles.

An even greater degree of duplicity was displayed by the German government over its efforts to hide the extent of its rearmament. This duplicity had begun long before Hitler came to power but rearmament under the Nazis was on a much greater scale.[10] The democratic states were aware of this and concerned not only about the expansion of the German regular forces but also about the growth of the para-military SA and SS. When the French ambassador questioned German officials about these organisations, they admitted that the SA had two million members but claimed that it was a non-military organisation.[11] Similarly Hitler told the British Ambassador,

> they are an inseparable component part of the political system of the National Socialist Revolution . . . They include some 2½ million men ranging from the 18th year to extreme age. Their only task is . . . to prevent for ever the return of the communist peril.[12]

The German authorities realised that Britain and France were aware that they were infringing the disarmament provisions of the Treaty of Versailles on a grand scale. The French Ambassador in Berlin told the German Foreign Minister that,

> they knew from numerous reports received by the French authorities from Germany to what extent the military training of the entire youth was being carried out and arms manufacture was being increased.[13]

Neurath told the ambassador that such reports were unreliable and that he knew nothing about rearmament. His reply was, to say the least, disingenuous since the military leaders had informed the Foreign Ministry on many occasions of their evasions of the treaties.[14] But it was not until later that Hitler reversed his policy and began to publicise the extent of his rearmament in selected areas. His policy then was to exaggerate the extent of his power in order to browbeat the democracies into giving way to his demands.[15] Even then he continued to dangle the prospect of disarmament before the democratic peoples in order to persuade them that he wanted a peaceful Europe.

The results of this policy were visible almost to the outbreak of war itself. When the British Prime Minister, Neville Chamberlain, met Hitler in Munich in September 1938 to decide the fate of Czechoslovakia, Chamberlain turned the conversation towards disarmament and mentioned the possibility of banning bomber aircraft. Hitler pointed out that, if only one major power, such as Japan or the Soviet Union, refused to sign an agreement of that sort, it would be unacceptable. Alternatively he suggested that states might agree not to carry out bombing raids more than 20 miles behind the front line in any war.[16] If the general public had been privy to these discussions, some would no doubt have been surprised that Chamberlain still considered it worthwhile to discuss disarmament with a man so obviously bent on changing the *status quo* and expanding his forces. As Winston Churchill had put it some years before,

> Germany is arming fast and no one is going to stop her. No one proposes a preventive war to stop Germany breaking the Treaty of Versailles. She is going to arm . . . The spirit of aggressive nationalism was never more rife in Europe and the world.[17]

Many would also have believed that Hitler's reluctance to ban bombers stemmed from his desire to use strategic bombers against his enemies. We now know that this was not so. Hitler's proposal to limit bombers to the battlefield fitted perfectly with the German policy of building an air force of ground support aircraft, such as the Stuka, which were designed to provide support for the troops of the German Army moving along the ground.[18]

The Luftwaffe was not planning to destroy enemy cities far behind the front line, partly because it felt that such strategic bombing attacks had not been successful in Spain. Thus, it could accept proposals of the sort that Hitler was advancing. It was Chamberlain's proposal that was at variance with his country's strategy. Even though Britain was now putting greater emphasis on fighters to protect the home base against air attack, the Royal Air Force had for many years seen one of its central roles in the event of a great war as the strategic bombing of enemy cities. Thus, the construction of bombers still took up much of its rearmament effort[19] and the prohibition of strategic bombing would have rendered much of this effort nugatory. Chamberlain was reacting to the widespread repugnance in England against the attacks on cities in Spain and China. The destruction of the Spanish town of Guernica had made a particular impact. He was also responding to the widespread fears that Germany would stage a 'knock-out' blow against London at the start of any war.[20] The general view was that the power of air attack was 'a hundred times greater than it was during the world war'.[21] Thus, as soon as Hitler came to power, British representatives in Germany showed particular sensitivity to increases in the size of the German air force.[22] The discrepancy between Chamberlain's proposal to ban bombers and British strategy was not, therefore, based on duplicity or realpolitik but on the conflicting pressures to which Chamberlain, like other democratic leaders, was subject. But, whilst dictators often have a clearer grasp of strategy than their democratic counterparts, they are not as Machiavellian as some would claim. Hitler could have caused Chamberlain a good deal of embarrassment in 1938 by accepting his proposal to ban long-range bombers.

Japan

The cynicism of Hitler's approach to disarmament in Europe was matched by the cynicism of the Japanese in Asia. The Japanese government called for the abolition of aircraft carriers and capital ships in the certain knowledge that its proposals would be rejected. What the Japanese navy really wanted — as the Germans wanted in Europe — was the ending of the legal restrictions on their force levels. By advocating radical disarmament measures, the Japanese gave a thin veneer to their anti-disarmament stance. The Chief of the Navy, General Fushimi, told the Japanese Emperor,

> Capital ships are the nucleus of seaborne military power. The complete abolition of these would be unprofitable from the standpoint of maintaining our position as a great naval power . . . our real intention is not to bring about the realization of this proposal. But we will propose this, in case the situation demands it, in order to strengthen the Empire's demands. We recognise that the possibility of realizing the complete abolition of capital ships is extremely small in view of England and United States' past demands.[23]

In the face of such cynicism was it possible to negotiate arms control or disarmament agreements with the dictatorships? The answer to the question as always goes back to the political roots of tensions. Hitler would have agreed to any treaty which facilitated the revision of the Versailles settlement. In particular he would have accepted a measure which reduced French power to the same level as Germany's. He wanted to achieve as many as possible of his revisionist aims without going to war but, if he had to fight, certain types of agreement, reducing the military power of the 'satisfied' states, could aid his victory. Similarly the Japanese government's aim was to seize Chinese territory and it would have accepted an agreement which reduced US and British power and made the conquest of China easier.

The issue then was not so much whether the democracies could negotiate a disarmament agreement with the dictators, but whether they accepted their revisionist aims. Since Hitler and the Japanese military authorities recognised that this was unlikely, they saw the disarmament negotiations and proposals as a way of dividing their potential enemies and weakening their armaments. The most idealistic of proposals worked to the advantage of the least idealistic of countries.

Notes

1. *Documents on German Foreign Policy 1918-1945*, Series C, Volume 1, HMSO, London, 1957, no. 9, p. 20. (hereafter DGFP).
2. DGFP, no. 226, p. 409, Minutes of the Conference of Ministers, 12 May 1933.
3. DGFP, no. 283, p. 516, Nadolny to the Foreign Ministry, 3 June 1933.
4. DGFP, nos. 200 and 202, pp. 365 and 368, Nadolny to the Foreign Ministry, 29 April 1933, and Neurath's reply, 2 May 1933.
5. DGFP, no. 447, p. 836, Neurath in Geneva to the Foreign Ministry, 24 September 1933.
6. DGFP, no. 466, p. 871, memorandum by Neurath in Geneva, 28 September 1933.
7. DGFP, Series C, Vol 11, p. 1. Proclamation to the German nation.
8. DGFP, no. 268, p. 508, ambassador in France to the Foreign Ministry, 19 February 1934.
9. DGFP, no. 277, p. 528, German ambassador in Rome to the Foreign Ministry, 24 February 1934.
10. See Chapter 10 below.
11. DGFP, no. 100, p. 174, memorandum by Bulow, 5 December 1933.
12. DGFP, no. 117, p. 198, Hitler to Phipps, 11 December 1933.
13. DGFP, Vol. 1, no. 360, p. 649, memorandum by Neurath, 13 July 1933.
14. DGFP, Vol. 11, no. 39, p. 61, Blomberg to the Foreign Ministry, 1 November 1933.
15. Lord Vansittart, *The Mist Procession*, Hutchinson, London, 1958, pp. 476-7.
16. *Documents on British Foreign Policy, 1919-1939, Third Series, Vol 2*,

HMSO, London, 1949, no. 1228, p. 636, Note of a conversation between the Prime Minister and Herr Hitler, 30 September 1938.

17. H. Montgomery Hyde, *British Air Policy Between the Wars, 1919-1939*, Heinemann, London, 1976, p. 299.

18. The Luftwaffe flirted with strategic bombers; see R.J. Overy, 'From "Uralbomber" to "Amerikabomber"', *Journal of Strategic Studies*, September 1978.

19. See Hyde, *British Air Policy*. See also R.J. Overy, *The Air War 1939-1945*, Europa, London, 1980, ch. 1.

20. Uri Bialer, *The Shadow of the Bomber*, Royal Historical Society, London, 1980.

21. *What would be the character of a New War?*, Gollancz, London, 1933, p. 21 passim.

22. DGFP, Vol. 11, no. 99, p. 173, memorandum by the Foreign Minister, 5 December 1933.

23. S. Pelz, *Road to Pearl Harbor*, Harvard, 1974, pp. 62-3.

7 THE SOVIET STANCE

Soviet security policy would appear to run parallel to that followed by Germany in the 1930s, at least in the secrecy with which it surrounds its armaments and the way that it pursues its interests single-mindedly in the negotiations. In analytical terms Soviet comments on security are often much more clear-headed than those coming from their democratic counterparts.

The Russians and their allies have been justifiably scathing about Western claims that a balance of power was the ideal way to preserve peace. On a number of occasions in the 1950s Soviet spokesmen at the UN attacked the Washington Naval Treaty on the grounds that it produced a balance of power in Asia and led to the Second World War.

> History can produce numerous examples to refute the argument that the principle of a balance of power and a system for the reduction of armaments based on that principle can ensure peace.[1]

Instead the Soviets advocated much more far-reaching disarmament measures. When Mr Khrushchev called for GCD in 1959, Czech spokesmen argued that 'the theory of the so-called balance in armaments had proved harmful to peace which could only be guaranteed by disarmament'. Similarly, when the Polish government called for the establishment of an NWFZ in Central Europe, its spokesmen argued that 'the concept of the balance of power was a highly elusive one which had been responsible for countless wars'.[2] Whatever the value of the concrete proposals put forward by the East Europeans, their suspicions of balance of power notions were, as we have already seen, fully justified. In recent years, however, their stance has been less clear cut and they have argued that there is an approximate military balance between East and West and that this is beneficial to the maintenance of peace. They may, therefore, have rightly come to see that it is mutual terror which currently preserves peace whatever the state of the military balance.

The Interwar Period

Before they seized power in 1917 the Bolsheviks had denounced disarmament measures as futile, whilst the bourgeois states were still in existence, but in 1922 they summoned a disarmament conference in Moscow. Poland, Estonia, Latvia and Finland attended and, as they were so often to do in the future, the Russians opened the conference by making a far-reaching disarmament proposal which they undoubtedly expected the other states to reject.[3] Once the other states had dismissed the idea of reducing their land forces by 75 per cent within two years, the Soviet government then revealed its real aims. It said that Russian forces had already been reduced to 800,000 men and would be reduced to 600,000 if the other countries represented in Moscow introduced comparable cuts. Agreement could still not be reached, largely because of controversies between the Russians and Poles. However, despite this failure, the Russians reduced their forces to 562,000 within two years. The probability therefore seems to be that they no longer felt sufficiently threatened by the democratic countries to consider it worthwhile maintaining such large forces. Having decided on reductions they hoped to persuade neighbouring states to follow suit.

The other Soviet disarmament proposals put forward in the interwar period were largely of the presentational type, designed to persuade the Western public that the Soviet Union was essentially peace-loving. In 1927, the Soviet Premier, Rykov, proposed 'that standing armies be completely abolished [and] that war industry be done away with'.[4] However, when a Soviet representative was sent to Geneva to present the Soviet proposals, he told newsmen that the Soviet Union, 'never concealed its disbelief in the willingness and ability of capitalist countries to abolish the system of wars among nations and consequently to achieve disarmament'.[5] Of course, if Soviet proposals for total disarmament had been accepted, the Russians would have dominated the European states by the size of their police and internal security forces. They would also still have been free to excite revolutions in the democracies, and the other states would have been in a weaker position to put them down. Soviet proposals were disingenuous but they were congruent with Soviet security interests.

Postwar Proposals

Soviet disarmament proposals in the late 1940s and 1950s once again reflected their views about their strength and weakness. Russian delegates to the UN's disarmament committees concentrated on nuclear disarmament proposals in order to try to limit the US lead in nuclear weapons. On 19 June 1946 Mr Gromyko presented a treaty to the UN imposing a ban on the production, storage and employment of nuclear weapons.[6] At the same time, the Russians opposed the US Baruch plan, which would have brought about verified nuclear disarmament by placing all nuclear establishments under international control, because they said it was intended 'to give the American monopolies total ownership and world control of atomic materials, fuels and developments'.[7] Instead the Russians suggested that nuclear weapons should be banned immediately and unconditionally. They also said that they were prepared to accept some degree of inspection on their territories to ensure that this was being carried out. But they were hazy about the nature of the organisation which would perform the inspection and they insisted that it should be controlled by the Security Council so that they could veto any activities of which they disapproved. Otherwise, 'the "suspicions" of the Western and pro-Western members of an international control commission would unquestionably be directed in the first instance towards those areas of the Soviet Union which were marked in white on the Pentagon's maps'.[8]

Secrecy was a significant weapon for the Soviet Union and a major advantage it held over the Western states. The West was prepared to negotiate on nuclear weapons where it possessed an unquestioned lead if, in return, the Russians reduced their conventional forces and gave up some of their secrecy.[9] But this they were never prepared to do.[10]

Through the 1950s, apart from making far-reaching proposals for nuclear disarmament, the Russians concentrated their criticisms on US military bases in foreign countries.[11] Nor was this very surprising, until the development of intercontinental bombers and ICBMs it was on these bases that the US Strategic Air Command was located. On the other hand, the Russians claimed that they 'had no military bases in the territory of other States. The very small number of troops which [the Soviet Union] maintained in Hungary and Romania were there in accordance with the peace treaties only in order to secure the Soviet Army's lines of communication'.[12] Soviet representatives also argued that it was not the total size of a country's armed forces which determined whether or not they were a threat to peace since

> those states having smaller amounts of effectives but, nevertheless, possessing tremendous naval and air armadas, as well as strings of military bases in foreign territories in the immediate vicinity of the territory of other States, were much more dangerous in their defence

machinery than those other States which had their armies situated inside their country.[13]

Western spokesmen responded by denying that foreign military bases were an intrinsic threat to peace, as the Russians claimed.[14] They also contended that the prohibition of foreign military bases would not hinder the Soviet Union with its vast territories but would severely reduce the military power of the West.

Representatives of NATO and the Warsaw Pact met in Geneva in November and December 1958 to discuss ways of reducing the danger of a surprise attack. The Western delegates concentrated on the indications which would show that particular weapons systems were being readied for war.[15] The Russians did make certain constructive suggestions for reducing the danger of a surprise attack in Europe, including the establishment of control posts at major ports, railway junctions and main roads. However, Soviet representatives linked this proposal with their campaign to prevent Germany acquiring nuclear weapons. They also claimed that 'flights of aircraft with atomic and hydrogen weapons on board over the territories of foreign states and over the open seas constitute a serious threat to world peace'.[16] Thus, the Conference rapidly became deadlocked and was apparently not even able to agree on an agenda.

It seems most unlikely that the Russians ever seriously expected the United States voluntarily to abandon its foreign military bases, at least without very large reductions in Soviet force-levels. However, constant Soviet criticisms of such bases might have stirred up resentment in Western Europe and elsewhere against the US bases there. Such a presence was historically anomalous. Traditionally the existence of foreign bases on a country's territory was the prelude to its loss of independence. Thus, it was by no means certain in the 1950s that the Europeans would not turn against their US protectors, as General de Gaulle was to show by taking France out of NATO's military structure in 1966. Similarly, Soviet attacks on the whole idea of having military alliances were, no doubt, directed at the European public rather than at the men in power. The Russians repeatedly claimed that they would disband the Warsaw Pact if NATO were dissolved, relying on the fact that the Warsaw Pact was a façade behind which they controlled Eastern Europe through the Red Army. The Russians attempted also to stir up Third World hatred of NATO by calling it 'an aggressive organisation designed to suppress popular movements and to secure world hegemony for itself'.[17] Such attacks achieved some success and many Third World countries joined in Soviet criticisms of Western alliances.

Foreign military bases were of most concern to the Soviet Union when the US deterrent was based on medium-range bombers and missiles. Thus, they argued that such bases were inherently threatening but, when they believed that they had a lead in ICBMs in the late 1950s, they firmly defended these weapons against the charge that they were aggressive or destabilising.[18] Conversely, Western spokesmen argued that ICBMs should be banned whilst they were still in the embryonic stage. The Russians retorted that the 'United States was proposing the prohibition of inter-continental rockets, which could only be used against its territory by way of retaliation, while retaining the advantages it derived from the military bases surrounding the Soviet Union and other socialist countries'.[19] Moreover, it was nuclear weapons that must be banned and not the rockets and aircraft which could serve useful and scientific purposes.

The Russians were frank about their hostility to foreign military bases and Western alliances, just as they were frank about their support for ICBMs when the October 1957 launching of Sputnik appeared to have given them a lead in this field. In this case, therefore, their disarmament proposals merely provided corroborative evidence of the areas about which they felt concern or confidence. Soviet spokesmen were much more cautious about admitting their fear of Western technology, although this fear was reflected in their disarmament proposals. The Soviet representative told the UN in 1962 that his country was by no means backward in military technology:

> for a number of years the West had cultivated a picture of the Soviet Union as a country which, being technically backward, was obliged to rely on numerical strength and conventional arms. It was claimed that the West was obliged to counter Soviet conventional superiority with nuclear arms. Such arguments were ridiculous as was shown by the Soviet Union's well known successes in science and technology. The Soviet Union's armed forces had all the most modern types of equipment at their disposal.[20]

Despite such boasts, Soviet representatives had made repeated proposals for limitations on military research and development. Western spokesmen pointed out both the difficulty of ensuring that such curbs were being upheld and of preventing advances in civilian technology from being applied to war. Almost all the major advances in twentieth-century military technology have been closely related to parallel developments in the civilian sphere, from aircraft to tanks and from chemical and nuclear weapons to space research and ICBMs.

In recent years the Russians have looked for more indirect ways of slowing the pace of Western technological advance. In particular, they called in 1975 for the prohibition of the development of new weapons of mass destruction.[21] Asked to explain what new weapons they had in mind, they took refuge in references to infrasonic weapons and to lasers. Western spokesmen pointed out that neither of these were likely to wreak mass destruction in the near future. But, when NATO began to consider the possibility of replacing some of its tactical nuclear warheads with reduced blast neutron weapons, the Russians claimed that these were the very sort of new weapons which they wished to ban.[22] Thus, they charged that the West was hampering the progress of disarmament by developing such weapons. The East also supported moves by the Committee on Disarmament at Geneva to monitor weapons under development to ensure that no new weapons of mass destruction were produced. Unfortunately, since the Russians publish little or no information about the weapons which they have under development, all the weapons considered by the Committee would be Western ones.

A major aim of Soviet disarmament policy since 1945 has been to prevent or to hinder the rearmament of West Germany, because of Soviet perceptions of the fundamental military strength of the Germans and therefore of the potential threat which they represent. East European spokesmen constantly warned that German 'militarism' was reviving.[23] Thus, when the rearmament of Germany was under consideration in NATO in 1954, the Soviet Union immediately advanced a series of disarmament proposals which would have hampered such moves. The Canadian representative at the UN pointed out that the timing of the Soviet Union's proposals 'suggests that the men in the Kremlin may have their eye rather on debates elsewhere – in London, in Paris – concerning the unity and defence programmes of Western Europe rather than on the desirability of a disarmament programme in itself'.[24]

Eastern bloc proposals for the establishment of a Central European NWFZ in 1958[25] were also largely aimed at neutralising West German power and preventing the stationing of US tactical nuclear weapons in West German territory. The Russians believed that such weapons threatened their superiority in manpower. Western spokesmen argued that the establishment of NWFZs should not upset the existing balance of power and that they should be part of a general agreement, not a prelude to it. Some years later when the possibility of NATO establishing a multilateral nuclear force was under discussion, Eastern bloc spokesmen warned that it would encourage nuclear proliferation and give the West Germans access to nuclear weapons. To gain Third World support the Russians argued that 'the creation of a unified NATO nuclear force would inevitably tend to increase imperialist and neo-colonialist pressures on the liberated peoples of the world and those still struggling for their liberation'.[26] Such claims struck a responsive chord and Ghana's spokesman at the UN said that he 'was alarmed at the prospect that Portugal, which was waging a ruthless colonial war in Africa with the help of its NATO allies, was to be associated with the use of nuclear weapons through the creation of a NATO multilateral force'.[27]

Eastern bloc disarmament negotiations have, therefore, provided a running commentary on the Soviet Union's perceptions of its strength and weakness. In particular, they have concentrated on the threat from a resurgent Germany and from Western technology. For much of the 1950s US bases and the missiles and bombers deployed on them were seen as the main danger to the Soviet Union. Subsequently, this threat was transferred to the Western Polaris and ICBM force, a transition marked by Soviet attacks on Western plans to locate submarines in the Mediterranean. In one of its most vitriolic notes the Soviet Union told the US government in May 1963 that 'the replacement of US fixed missile bases by floating ones' was inherently threatening and warned that 'the countries in which their submarines are based, permanently or from time to time, would expose themselves to the greatest danger'.[28] Thus, the Russians proposed that the Mediterranean should become a nuclear weapons free zone in which they and the other nuclear weapon states would refrain from sending nuclear weapons. If this were to happen, the Soviet government promised to give 'reliable guarantees that, in the event of any military complications, the area of the Mediterranean sea will be considered as outside the sphere of use of nuclear weapons'.

The 1963 proposal was significant because it was the first time that the Russians had made a serious naval arms control proposal since 1945. Although the West had dominated the world's oceans up to that time, such dominance had not been perceived by the Russians as a threat because the Soviet Union, unlike the West, was not dependent upon foreign trade for its survival. But the weakness of the Soviet pretension to be a world power had been exposed by the Cuba crisis in September and October 1962. The Soviet decision to withdraw its nuclear weapons from Cuba, together with the Western decision to put a significant portion of its deterrent force into submarines, concentrated Soviet attention on the sea. The Soviet government has subsequently therefore made periodic naval arms control proposals. Presentationally the Soviet Union has advantages: any agreement which tended to equalise Soviet and Western naval power would favour the Soviet Union because the Soviet Navy is a luxury while naval power is a vital necessity for the West. Hence, the Russians can make apparently reasonable proposals which would be extremely dangerous from the Western point of view. Moreover, the Soviet Union would claim that it is a Mediterranean power by virtue of its Black Sea coastline. Thus, any proposal to remove 'foreign' navies from the Mediterranean could be expected to remove US but not Soviet naval forces, while any proposal to limit the presence of nuclear missile-carrying submarines in the Mediterranean would effect the West but leave the Soviet Union free to send similar submarines to the Caribbean and to other areas close to the United States should the increasing range of its submarine based missiles not make it unnecessary to do so.

Strategic Arms Limitation Talks

The Russians rejected President Johnson's original proposal for a freeze on strategic delivery vehicles in January 1964, largely because the United States was so far ahead in the nuclear arms race at that time.[29] However, Washington continued to be concerned about the development of strategic weapons, not least because the Soviet Union appeared to be determined to build up its anti-ballistic missile defences (ABM). Thus, the Americans continued to press the idea of negotiations and in May 1968, when they 'were in the process of achieving parity or approximate parity with the United States' in offensive systems, the Russians responded favourably. The talks were further delayed by the Soviet invasion of Czechoslovakia and by the replacement of President Johnson by President Nixon and it was not until November 1969 that negotiations began.

It rapidly became clear that the main Soviet aim in the negotiations was to limit US deployment of multiple independently targeted re-entry vehicles (MIRV). On the other hand, the main aim of the US administration was to limit Soviet deployment of heavy missiles, such as the SS 9, because many felt that they were a threat to the existing US land-based ICBMs. The Russians also made clear their concern about US forward based systems in Europe, including carrier and land based aircraft, which could attack the Soviet Union with nuclear weapons. The Russians wanted these to be described as strategic because they could hit the Soviet homeland, whilst the Soviet force of medium and intermediate range ballistic missiles would be excluded because it was aimed at Western Europe and not the United States. Soviet interest in halting the US MIRV programme was natural because it was widely known that this was the main US strategic programme at that time. There were some in the US government who would have liked to restrict MIRV deployment because of the twist to the arms spiral which it would give. However, a ban on MIRV development and deployment could only be verified by satellites if it took place before the Russians began testing MIRVs. Once the MIRVed missiles had been tested, on-site inspection would be necessary to ensure that they had not been installed and the Soviet Union would not permit such measures. Because of these difficulties and because of divisions within the US administration, the Americans decided to abandon proposals for MIRV limitations after the second round of SALT which lasted from April to August 1970.

Despite this setback, Soviet interest in reaching a SAL agreement increased, particularly during the fifth round of talks which began in July 1971, because of the improvement in Sino-American relations which took place when the Secretary of State, Dr Kissinger, visited Peking at that time. Thus, the Russians accepted a separate limit on the number of heavy missiles which either side would be permitted to deploy. However, they insisted on being granted some advantage in numbers of submarines and submarine-launched missiles because they had no bases in foreign countries and, therefore, it took longer for their boats to reach their launching points. Once this point had been conceded at the seventh and final session, it was the differing assessments of the number of boats possessed by the Soviet Union which caused most difficulty. The Russians claimed that they had 768 missile tubes already operational on their boats, whilst the United States claimed that they only had 640. Because numbers were to be frozen this dichotomy caused considerable difficulty but eventually a compromise was reached on the assumption that the Russians had 740 tubes operational.[30]

The negotiations were completed in May 1972. They had clearly demonstrated the interaction between political and strategic developments and perceptions. Soviet willingness to participate reflected its desire to be seen as a Great Power on a level with the United States in the nuclear as in other fields. The Russians were also undoubtedly concerned that US technology was likely to nullify any strategic gains which they had made in the 1960s. In the event, the MIRV gap proved shorter-lived than many Russians must have feared before the negotiations began. But it was replaced in the second half of the 1970s by a potential cruise missile gap. On their side, the Americans continued to fear that improvements in the accuracy of the Soviet ICBM force would make US land based missiles vulnerable to a Soviet first strike. In one sense each Super Power's perceptions of its own weakness in particular areas increased its motive for reaching an arms control agreement. On the other hand, such perceptions also increased each side's suspicions — suspicions which were undoubtedly enhanced on the Soviet side by the US rapprochement with China.

Conclusion

Is the problem faced by the democracies in negotiating with the Soviet Union the same as the problem they faced when dealing with Germany and Japan in the 1930s? Can disarmament agreements only be negotiated if they facilitate the Kremlin's revisionist aims? Technically there are many similarities because democracies, swept by the ebb and flow of public opinion, are faced by closed societies about whose decision-making processes nothing is known. Politically Soviet aims are even more unlimited than those of Germany and Japan in the 1930s. In theory the Kremlin is committed to transforming the world into a communist 'Utopia'. However, in practice Soviet leaders know, after their experience with China and Yugoslavia, that a world of communist states would not necessarily be under their control, that it would be highly militarised because of the ability of totalitarian states to expand their armed forces without popular resistance and thus that it might actually threaten their interests. A communist world would also be very violent. Since the emergence of a Soviet bloc in 1945 there have been five full-scale invasions by one communist state of another, one prolonged border conflict (China and the Soviet Union) and two extensive guerrilla wars (in Afghanistan and Kampuchea). The level of such violence has increased in direct proportion to the number of communist states and appears very largely to be motivated by ideological feuds and fanaticism.

   Despite all this, Soviet leaders may still hope to achieve a communist world but they seem to have recognised that it cannot be achieved through a war between the Great Powers because of the threat of nuclear destruction, though they continue to favour civil and guerrilla wars when these lead to the victory of the 'progressive' forces. Within these limitations they are prepared to negotiate measures designed to reduce the possibility of war with NATO. One writer has argued that the Russians see all disarmament measures as essentially political; 'thus to the Russians arms control in Europe was not a relatively apolitical process of stabilizing the balance of deterrence, as the concept of MBFR suggested, but an attempt to secure Russia's political goals via symbolic reductions in NATO-WPO forces.'[31] If this is the view of Soviet statesmen it reveals a much more profound view of East-West relations than the one espoused by many Western statesmen. Support for this analysis of Soviet motives is given by the Kremlin's approach towards other totalitarian states, such as Nazi Germany and communist China, where the Russians have not negotiated for arms control agreements but for general treaties of friendship or alliance. On the other hand, this view is directly the opposite of what Soviet leaders say. Over and over again in public they argue that the arms race itself is a cause of war and that it must be halted by arms control agreements. Such arguments may be nothing but cynical ploys to strengthen Western unilateralism but, as we have seen, the Russians have very often advocated technical arms control measures which would strengthen their own position. They were apparently interested in nuclear arms control in the 1950s because the West was ahead in that area, not because an agreement would have symbolised an improvement in East-West relations.

In one respect it might be easier for the West to negotiate agreements with the Soviet Union than vice versa. The Kremlin has a much clearer idea of its strategic interests than its Western equivalents and it is not influenced by the ebb and flow of public opinion. Its proposals are thus almost entirely predictable. They take a very hard look at every deal offered and if it is in their interests they accept it. In contrast Western governments are pushed about by the tides of idealism which make them advance proposals and then draw back. Thus in 1955 the USA suddenly reserved its position on all the disarmament proposals which the West had made in recent years. Similarly during the SAL talks it was constantly changing its position on ABMs, MIRVs and other weapons.[32] The democracies lack the hard-headed, clear-cut strategic ideas which shape Soviet foreign policy in general and its arms control policy in particular.

Notes

1. 699 meeting of the UN First Committee, 25 October 1954. See also the Soviet statement at the 602 meeting, 15 April 1953.
2. See the Czech statement at the 1027 meeting, 10 October 1959, and the Polish statement at the 1341 meeting, 19 November 1953.
3. R.W. Lambert, *Soviet Disarmament Policy, 1922-1931, US Arms Control and Disarmament Agency* (ACDA), Washington, 1964, p. 4.
4. Ibid., p. 29.
5. Ibid.
6. *Documents on Disarmament 1945-1959*, Vol. 1, Department of State, Washington, 1960, p. 20.
7. 580 meeting of the UN First Committee, 20 March 1953.
8. 1254 meeting of the UN First Committee, 23 October 1962.
9. See, for example, D. Acheson, *Present at the Creation*, Hamish Hamilton, London, 1969, p. 581.
10. See Note 7 supra.
11. 982 meeting of the UN First Committee, 12 November 1958.
12. 676 meeting of the UN First Committee, 26 November 1953.
13. 670 meeting of the UN First Committee, 19 November 1953.
14. 673 meeting of the UN First Committee, 23 November 1953.
15. *Documents on Disarmament 1945-1959*, Vol. 2, Department of State, Washington, 1960, p. 1230 passim.
16. Loc. cit., p. 1227.
17. 602 meeting of the UN First Committee, 15 April 1953.
18. 982 meeting of the UN First Committee, 12 November 1958.
19. Ibid.
20. 1279 meeting of the UN First Committee, 16 November 1962.
21. 'Weapons of doom just talk', *Guardian*, 12 March 1976.
22. 42 meeting of the UN First Committee at the 33 Session of the General Assembly, 17 November 1978.
23. 825 meeting of the UN First Committee, 21 January 1957.
24. 688 meeting of the UN First Committee, 13 October 1954.
25. J.H. Barton and L.D. Weiler (eds.), *International Arms Control: Issues and Agreements*, Stanford University Press, 1976, p. 252.
26. 1355 meeting of the UN First Committee, 18 October 1965.
27. 1366 meeting of the UN First Committee, 27 October 1965.
28. *Documents on Disarmament 1963*, ACDA, Washington, 1964, p. 187 passim.
29. Barton and Weiler, *International Arms Control*, ch. nine.
30. Loc. cit.
31. R. Ranger, 'MBFR: political or technical arms control', *Journal of the Air Force Department Society*, 1975.
32. Barton and Weiler, *International Arms Control*, pp. 76 and 179 passim.

8 THIRD WORLD SECURITY POLICY

Introduction

Over the last 15 years the arms control negotiations have become increasingly bifurcated. On the one hand, there has been the hard-headed bargaining between East and West on limiting strategic arms (SALT), on banning all nuclear weapons tests (CTBT) and on force reductions in Europe (MBFR); while, on the other hand, the negotiations at the UN and at the Committee on Disarmament (CD) in Geneva have taken on an increasingly North-South character. The more successful the East-West negotiations became in the 1960s and 1970s, the more the Third World was excluded from this arcane sphere. Third World countries want the East-West negotiations to succeed but suspect the collusion between the Great Powers which this has involved, and they have their own ideas on security and on the way the East-West negotiations should proceed.

There is, of course, a sharp contrast between Third World advocacy of East-West disarmament and arms control negotiations and the virtual absence of such negotiations amongst Third World states themselves. Only in Latin America have the developing countries negotiated regional arms control agreements. Third World governments and commentators would explain this discrepancy by arguing that the Great Powers alone are a threat to world peace, even if it is in the Third World that most wars take place. But the most important reasons for the discrepancy are the virtual absence of public pressure for arms control in the developing states and the desire of these countries to increase their relative power *vis-à-vis* the developed world. Third World statements on arms control and disarmament incorporate most of the conceptual weaknesses discussed in the previous section. Above all they fail to give adequate consideration to the political roots of East-West tensions. They find it easy to criticise the Great Powers' armaments. They call for the most far-reaching disarmament measures but fail to show how these can be achieved in the face of existing tensions.

The success of the East-West negotiations depends on the ability of the Americans and Russians to limit their competition and to work together. But at the UN and in the CD they are competitors for the support of the rest of the world. Consequently they behave there rather like democratic politicians trying to woo a vociferous but gullible electorate without changing their fundamental positions by promises of action to come and protestations of good intentions. The Russians have an advantage in this competition because the non-aligned states have attacked almost every aspect of Western strategy as it has evolved since the Second World War, from permanent military bases in foreign countries, through military alliances, to the theory of deterrence and the professed desire to maintain a balance of power with the Soviet Union. In the 1950s the West was able, if it wished, to ignore such criticisms, but the growing UN voting power of the Third World and the threat to destroy or damage the barriers to nuclear proliferation give the non-aligned a bargaining counter in the negotiations.

Nevertheless, the debates between the Third World and the West have attracted little interest in Western circles. With rare exceptions Western academics have ignored Third World comments on security because the historical and other premises from which Third World writers are working have become increasingly alien to modern Western strategists. This lack of response has produced a justified feeling of frustration amongst the non-aligned, and Third World writers have responded with accusations that the 'military-industrial-intellectual complexes in the industrial nations are in the grip of an irrational cult which has engulfed them in a dangerous closed system of logic'.[1] This chapter seeks to expound the criticisms which Third World writers and statesmen have made of Western security policies and to assess the value of such criticisms. Inevitably it simplifies the varied and often conflicting arguments which Third World spokesmen have used and modified over the years, as indeed it simplifies the expositions which have been made of Western policies.

Nuclear Weapons

Criticisms of Western strategy almost invariably begin with an attack on Western nuclear policies. Third World governments, led by India, have exerted continuing pressure on the NWS to reduce and ultimately abolish their nuclear weapons. They maintain that they are

> alarmed by the threat to the very survival of mankind posed by the existence of weapons of mass destruction, particularly nuclear weapons

and that they are

> convinced that global catastrophe can only be averted by arresting and reversing the arms race and by the final elimination of all nuclear weapons and other means of mass destruction.[2]

Many Third World writers and statesmen have sought to deny that nuclear deterrence has been responsible for preserving peace between East and West since 1945. Criticisms of deterrence date from the early 1950s when Third World spokesmen at the UN, such as Krishna Menon, argued that 'it was not possible to frighten people into peace. Fear was the cause of war and armaments'.[3] The current attitude towards nuclear deterrence amongst Third World writers and academics is ambiguous; in most collections of Third World writings, some commentators deny the effectiveness of nuclear deterrence, while others admit its effectiveness but deny its morality.[4] Many Third World writers argue that Russia never intended to attack the West and that this was proved by the fact that it did not carry out such an attack when it had developed nuclear weapons of its own,[5] while others believe that

> . . . if the world of the Cold War stands discredited . . . today it is mainly as a result of the Soviet policies and practices in the field of diplomacy and foreign policy . . . and not, as the West would like us to believe, due to any balance of terror or nuclear deterrence.[6]

For most Third World countries nuclear disarmament is far more desirable than conventional. Third World countries could well be seriously damaged by the fall-out from a nuclear war even though they might be opposed to the ends for which it was fought. As the Yugoslav representatives pointed out at the UN in the 1950s

> the smaller powers, like Yugoslavia, which had no weapons of mass destruction, would nonetheless be annihilated by them if they were used . . . the free and peaceful development of small states could be safeguarded only by a system of collective security.[7]

Consequently, at Third World conferences, such as Bandung, the developing countries did not wish conventional disarmament to be linked with the prohibition of nuclear arms.[8] They also began to formulate the notion of zones of peace and subsequently of NWFZ which were intended to exclude the East-West Cold War from the Third World.

Third World states claim that they are threatened both directly and indirectly by nuclear weapons. Thus, they have persistently tried to persuade the NWS to state that they would not use their nuclear weapons, or failing this, that they would not use their nuclear weapons first or against a non-nuclear weapon state. In 1960 Ethiopia sponsored a resolution at the UN which called for the use of nuclear weapons to be made a crime under international law. The resolution won the support of most developing countries, including Ceylon which protested that the two military blocs 'seemed to feel that the extermination of the human race would be preferable to the victory of the opposing ideology'.[9] Subsequently the Third World states have sought both guarantees that the nuclear weapons states would come to their aid if they were attacked by another NWS, and assurances that the NWS would promise not to use, or to threaten to use, their nuclear weapons against them. Since the 1950s, when the proposal was first made by India, the Third World states have also pressed for a ban on nuclear weapon tests. They particularly resented the practice of testing nuclear weapons far from the homeland of the NWS. Preparations for French nuclear tests in the Sahara led to the condemnation of France by the UN General Assembly in 1959 and to proposals for the establishment of an African NWFZ. The Ceylonese representative at the UN warned that,

what the people of Africa would remember would be the fact that a European power had chosen an African territory in which to explode a bomb that might have dangerous consequences to the people of that territory.[10]

Soviet Views

On many of these issues the Russians supported the proposals put forward by the Third World. As we saw in the last chapter, through much of the 1950s they placed greater emphasis on nuclear than on conventional disarmament because their conventional forces were numerically stronger than those of the NATO countries and their nuclear forces were weaker. The Russians have never openly accepted the doctrine of nuclear deterrence[11] and it is a matter of controversy whether they see nuclear weapons as a deterrent or as another way of waging war. Like the non-aligned countries, the Russians have frequently called for the dissolution of military alliances because they control Eastern Europe through the Red Army, rather than co-ordinate it through the Warsaw Pact. They also claim that they have no bases on foreign territories,[12] though these claims seem to be based on a semantic quibble as much as on a disagreement about the facts. The Soviet Union has, however, parted company from the non-aligned and the West on anything which smacks of international control. On the other hand, perhaps because it takes a more cynical view of the proceedings, the Soviet Union has been much more effective than the West at producing disarmament 'initiatives' which appeal to the mass of Third World nations. Each year at the UN it unfolds an initiative of this sort; in 1973, for example, it called for a reduction of 10 per cent in the military budgets of the permanent members of the Security Council and for the allocation of some of the resources released to aid the developing countries.[13]

Only on the Nuclear Non-Proliferation Treaty does the Soviet Union stand shoulder to shoulder with the Western states, although even here the Russians would prefer the West to take the lead, because of the resentment caused by the Treaty in the Third World. According to much Third World literature the Treaty is based on the premise that

> while responsible powers, like the US, USSR, Britain and France and China can be safely entrusted with nuclear weapons, it is dangerous for Arabs and Israelis, Indians, Pakistanis and others to have such weapons.[14]

Sources of Tension

Collectively, Third World criticisms of Western policies on nuclear proliferation and other issues reflect a different view of the sources of tension in the world than the one held by many in the West. Commentators in the northern hemisphere frequently point out that it is in the southern hemisphere where violence is endemic and argue that the developed states frequently try to limit this violence and show an increasing reluctance to use force themselves.[15] On the other hand, in fora dominated by the Third World, such as the UN, the USA and Soviet Union are accused of carrying on an arms race which 'both reflects and aggravates international tensions, sharpens conflicts in various regions of the world, hinders the process of detente, exacerbates the differences between the opposing military alliances, jeopardizes the security of all states'.[16]

Thus, even where Third World commentators agree that most conflicts now occur in the southern hemisphere, they still maintain that the
Great Powers are responsible for these outbreaks of violence. For
example, one Indian writer has argued that the Great Powers,

> found it irresistible to feed and reinforce the regional roots of the
> South Asian conflict. The Great Power involvement was so deep and
> pervasive that one is led to believe that the Great Powers in pur-
> suance of their global and regional objectives would have invented a
> conflict in South Asia if none had existed.[17]

Hedley Bull, one of the few Western strategists who has taken Third
World writings on security seriously, has argued that the current arms
control negotiations will have to be modified considerably before the
gap between the North and the South can be narrowed. The non-
aligned

> see the emphasis on Soviet-American bilateral goals — in arms con-
> trol, in the treatment of security as the commanding value, in the
> preoccupation with the stabilization of the Great Power balance, in
> the efforts to control proliferation, and in the network of tacit
> understandings between the Great Powers — as part of the system of
> hegemony which they wish to break down in spite of the fact that
> they have nothing in mind with which to replace it.[18]

In fact, the developing countries are not as hostile to the current arms
control negotiations as this suggests. The aims of most of these negotiations (SALT, Test Ban, MBFR, ban on chemical weapons) are
endorsed by the Third World; their complaint is rather that the negotiations are not proceeding fast enough and that they are not asked to
participate. The successful achievement of any or all of these negotiations would not increase the relative power of the Super Powers, unless
it can be argued that chemical weapons are within the reach of any
state with a rudimentary chemical industry and that an effective ban on
such weapons would prevent the Third World balancing the nuclear
weapons of the Great Powers with their own chemical weapons.[19]
Only the Nuclear Non-Proliferation Treaty and the efforts to control
the conventional arms trade are designed to preserve the existing dis-
tribution of weaponry. The other negotiations are, and are generally
seen to be, attempts to tame the military power of the major states.
   Little can be done to satisfy those Third World countries which

deny that there is a Soviet threat to the West and therefore argue that the NATO states have no need for large defence forces. The evidence for such a threat cannot be proven from statements by East European defectors, or critics such as Solzhenitsyn or Djilas, since their evidence is automatically suspect; nor can it be deduced from Marxist doctrine which can be interpreted in as many ways as the Bible. But the threat seemed real enough in the West, after the absorption of Eastern Europe in the Soviet Empire, for the doctrine of nuclear deterrence to develop. As the 1954 British defence White Paper put it,

> if by some miscalculation in Communist policy or by deliberate design, a global war were to be forced upon us . . . it seems likely that such a war would begin with a period of intense atomic attacks lasting a relatively short time but inflicting great damage and destruction.[20]

Western statesmen were thus not deterred from threatening to use nuclear weapons because the Russians also possessed them. We cannot know whether such statements persuaded the Russians not to attack. They may have had a higher appreciation of the value of Western conventional weapons than some Western commentators, or they may never have intended to attack at all.

The Western Position

The Western states have also made major concessions to reduce the East-West arms race. In the 1950s they maintained a commanding lead in nuclear weapons in order to balance the perceived superiority of Soviet conventional forces in Europe. Western nuclear superiority was eroded in the 1970s when 'sufficiency', rather than superiority, was said to be the goal. This was a greater concession than is sometimes recognised; as we have seen, Western experience in the 1930s had demonstrated clearly that to allow a revisionist power to increase its conventional forces until it has achieved parity with the *status quo* powers is to court disaster. Soviet conventional superiority in the key area of Western Europe, together with its local nuclear superiority and parity with US strategic forces, places even more emphasis on the importance of nuclear deterrence.

However, Third World critics are right to point out that the near unanimity of Western strategists and governments on the value of nuclear deterrence is no proof of the validity of the doctrine and may indeed be dangerous. Both before the First World War and in the 1920s certain views on strategic matters were almost unquestioned and yet these views were totally discredited in the West within a decade of their ascendancy. Third World countries are nevertheless wrong to suggest that the West has accepted deterrence hastily and uncritically. In fact the idea was only accepted gradually after an intense public and official debate lasting over a decade − a debate which has to be refought each generation. The debate also encompassed the alternatives to deterrence, including the possibility of general and complete disarmament. But the probability of achieving this and of ensuring the stability of a disarmed world were generally agreed to be slight. As one Western commentator has written,

> the elimination of this potential [to use force] has been the object of disarmament studies throughout this century, and for some five years, between 1958 and 1963, the entire community of strategic thinkers concentrated their attention upon the problem, with regrettable lack of success . . . The innumerable studies devoted to the subject of disarmament [did little] more than reveal its complexity.[21]

Nuclear Assurances

The Western states have never tried to minimise the horrific nature of nuclear weapons. They have, however, tried to meet claims that the Third World states were directly threatened by such weapons. In response to Indian criticisms, Britain and France proposed in 1954 that the NWS should state that they

> regard themselves as prohibited in accordance with the Charter of the UN from the use of nuclear weapons except in defence against aggression.

Selwyn Lloyd, the British spokesman, explained that the prohibition was partial because,

> there can be no doubt that the possibility of the use of atomic weapons against him is a powerful deterrent to an aggressor.

The Russians rejected the Western proposal on the grounds that

> such a formula could itself offer a basis for sanctioning the use of atomic weapons on the pretext of defence against aggression when there was no such defence in reality.[22]

Krishna Menon also argued that such an assurance was valueless because all belligerents always believed that they were fighting for peace and liberty.

The suggestion that states would circumvent such an agreement by arguing that they were defending themselves against unprovoked attack or making some other excuse was undoubtedly justified. But this is true of any assurance of this type however it is phrased. In the desperate situation when the use of nuclear weapons would be considered as a possible option (for instance in the event of a successful Russian invasion of Western Europe) an assurance of any sort would be one of the least factors affecting the decisions of the NWS. That this fact is recognised by most states is demonstrated by two historical examples. In 1961 the East Europeans supported the Ethiopian proposal at the UN that the use of nuclear weapons should be declared a crime. However, just before the session, Khrushchev had given an interview to the *New York Times* in which he had said,

> let us assume that both sides were to promise not to employ nuclear weapons, but retained their stockpiles. What would happen if the imperialists unleashed war? In such a war if any side should feel it was losing, would it not use nuclear weapons to avoid defeat? It would undoubtedly use its nuclear bombs.[23]

Khrushchev's comments caused embarrassment amongst the Eastern bloc negotiators and were quoted by Western spokesmen to explain their opposition to the Third World's non-use resolution. The Russians replied that their leader's comments had been made in reply to a question about a unilateral non-use assurance which was true but irrelevant to the point at issue. As the Italian delegate pointed out,

> the Soviet Union was ready to vote in favour of a draft resolution which it did not intend to respect if it should prove contrary to its own interests.[24]

A second example of the real value which states give to such assurances by their potential enemies is provided by the Indian reaction to the Chinese nuclear bomb tests in the 1960s. From the start the Chinese gave precisely the sort of non-first-use assurance which the Indians had been incessantly demanding from the existing NWS, that 'at no time and in no circumstances would China be the first to use nuclear weapons'.[25] Neither the Indian public nor the Indian government appear to have given any credence to this statement.[26] Instead, the advocates of Indian nuclear weapons have used the Chinese nuclear programme to bolster their case, while the Indian government worked hard during the 1960s to obtain positive security guarantees from the other NWS that they would give aid in the event of a Chinese attack on India. The government also argued that the absence of a credible guarantee was one of the reasons why it could not sign the Nuclear Non-Proliferation Treaty. It is perfectly possible that the Indian government would have given more credence to a Western or a Soviet non-first-use assurance than to a Chinese one, but this only reinforces the point, an assurance by a friendly state is unnecessary, an assurance by a potential enemy is incredible.

Nevertheless, Third World countries, including India, have continued to press for nuclear assurances. To meet this pressure, the Russians, the British and Americans gave assurances at the UN Special Session on Disarmament in 1978 about the circumstances in which they would use nuclear weapons.[27] All three states said that they would not use nuclear weapons against states which had renounced the acquisition of such weapons. But the Russians added the additional proviso that such states should not have nuclear weapons on their territory, while the Western states said that they should not be engaged in an armed attack in association or alliance with a nuclear weapon state. The Russian formula seemed to be designed to discourage West European states from having US nuclear weapons on their territory, while the Western formula makes clear that the West might use nuclear weapons against any of the Warsaw Pact states in the event of an Eastern attack.

However, before the second UN Special Session on Disarmament, the Soviet position began to change. Mr Brezhnev announced in June 1982 'the USSR assumed the obligation not to be the first to use nuclear weapons'. This was a clear bid to win Third World support since Mr Brezhnev argued that 'a ban on the use of nuclear weapons . . . is espoused by the overwhelming majority of the countries of the world'. But the essence of the situation, of the factors which govern whether nuclear weapons would be used, has not changed since Mr Khrushchev's 1961 statement. As Mr Brezhnev himself noted ambiguously or threateningly in his June 1982 statement: 'in the conduct of its policy the Soviet Union will naturally continue to take into account how the other nuclear powers react'.[28]

In fact, although Third World states claim to be directly threatened by nuclear weapons, there is no evidence that they have been deterred from acting against an NWS by the fear of a nuclear attack. The Egyptians and Somalis have thrown large numbers of Russian advisers out of their territories and the Afghan guerrillas continue to resist Soviet forces; the North Vietnamese have defeated the Americans and continue their occupation of Kampuchea despite Chinese threats and attacks; and the Indonesians and Argentinians have fought the British without apparently losing much sleep about their danger from nuclear attack. Some might argue that these disputes were essentially peripheral but it is difficult to conceive of a case where the dispute between one of the existing NWS and a Third World state would be much less peripheral from the NWS's point of view. In anything like the present international climate, nuclear weapons are only of use for the Great Powers for threatening or fighting other nuclear weapon states. Political inhibitions against the use of nuclear weapons have become stronger over the years and the production of 'cleaner' or smaller nuclear weapons will not reverse this trend. However, while it is difficult to take the purported fears of a direct attack seriously, the fear of contamination from a nuclear war is a different story.

In the early postwar years NATO expected the Third World to accept as a matter of course the risks of radioactive contamination which would result from a Western nuclear response to a Soviet attack on West Europe. Many developing countries did publicly support Western deterrence policies. Venezuela told the UN that the

destructive power of atomic weapons had, it would seem, diminished the likelihood of their being used and had therefore made possible the coexistence of two antagonistic political and economic systems.[29]

Similarly Cuba maintained that

it was a grave error to affirm that nuclear weapons had not served to preserve the integrity and liberty of states, for recent history demonstrates that states and peoples which could not defend themselves had been reduced to slavery, while the countries possessing atomic weapons, and their allies, had remained free.[30]

Some states, such as Cuba and Iraq, changed their stance on these questions when radical regimes came to power, others, such as Yugoslavia, became more critical of Western strategy when their relations with the Soviet Union improved.

The Western position on the general question of nuclear deterrence is most easily defensible if the political and military preconceptions on which it is based are accepted; that the Soviet Union is inherently expansionist but can be deterred by a nuclear threat; that it is controlled by a politically and morally repugnant regime and that similar regimes have shown a high propensity to fight each other and to invade non-communist states; that its hostility to inspection on its territory shows a determination, or at least a propensity, to cheat on disarmament agreements; and that its conventional forces are maintained in such numbers and in a state of readiness for attack which the West cannot match conventionally in Europe.

However, some Third World writers have pointed out that the Western powers have been more often engaged in armed conflict since 1945 than the Russians and they have argued that this reflects their inherently greater expansionism. Dislike for the Soviet political system is less intense in the Third World than in the West, partly because most newly independent countries call themselves socialist, and partly because the prevalent attitude towards the rule of law and to democratic rights is closer in the Third World to Soviet than to Western practice. Because Third World countries are not directly involved in the East-West balance they often argue that the West should take greater risks in the interests of disarmament. They also argue that Western unwillingness to match Soviet conventional forces in Europe shows Western doubts about Soviet expansionism, rather than the preference of Western electorates for butter instead of guns. Thus, the political basis for Western defence policy is frequently not accepted in the developing countries.

The West was willing to put its point of view over and over again in international fora in the 1950s and early 1960s. In the late 1960s, as the process of detente developed, the West was no longer willing to explain its position at the UN. It was therefore asking non-members of the two main military alliances to risk contamination from a nuclear war for the sake of policies which it was no longer willing to defend. At the same time it became increasingly unwilling to point out the problems of verification and other difficulties in the way of disarmament, particularly in the nuclear field. In the 1950s the West had had no such inhibitions.[31]

The non-aligned position on verification was based on the assumption that the Russians could be trusted or that the risks of trusting them were less that the risks of nuclear deterrence. The Western nations rejected this advice but in the late 1960s and 1970s they also began to talk occasionally as if nuclear disarmament were possible in the foreseeable future. In his inaugural speech, President Carter pledged:

we will move this year a step towards our ultimate goal – the elimination of all nuclear weapons from this earth.[33]

Ten months later he told the UN that the US was willing to reduce its nuclear weapons by up to 50 per cent, 'then we will work for further reductions to a world truly free of nuclear weapons'. Such comments deliberately blur the distinction between nuclear bombs and their delivery systems and this ambiguity was repeated in Western papers submitted to the UN Special Session on Disarmament in May, 1978. However, reduction in nuclear warheads is even more difficult to verify than reductions in delivery systems and the Soviet Union has shown no sign of accepting the necessary measures. When the US suggested in the 1960s that there should be token (verified) reductions in nuclear warhead stocks, the Russians ignored this suggestion.[34]

Nuclear Proliferation

Third World states and commentators are given to arguing that if some nations should have nuclear weapons, all should do so in the name of equality.[35] This ignores the fact that most nations in the world will be incapable of producing nuclear weapons for the next 50 years and that there is therefore bound to be some degree of inequality in the spread of nuclear weapons, as indeed there is in every other sort of weapon. Moreover, while Third World countries argue that they would behave as rationally as the current nuclear powers if they processed nuclear weapons, their arguments ignore the technical differences between nuclear forces. In order to give new strategic nuclear forces the same stability as the existing ones, Third World states might not have to develop nuclear missile-carrying submarines or missiles in hardened silos, as the United States and the Soviet Union have done. But they would obviously have to make certain that their bombers or other delivery systems could not be knocked out in a first strike by enemy forces and they would have to develop fail-safe devices to prevent the unauthorised use of their nuclear weapons.

Countries building up nuclear forces should also recognise that during the build-up the incentive for any potential enemy to attack them is greatly increased. There was some political pressure on Western statesmen in the 1940s to use their nuclear weapons on the Soviet Union before the Russians acquired a similar capability. The Russians made their most direct threat against the British and French during the 1956 Suez operation before the European countries had acquired an effective retaliatory capability. Similarly, stories of Russian plans to attack the Chinese in the early stages of their nuclear programme derive their plausibility from 'the urge to pre-empt'.[36]

In an international forum such as the UN it is impossible to suggest that the likelihood of internal unrest, *coup d'état* or civil war varies from one state to another, and therefore a realistic discussion of the danger of nuclear proliferation is impossible. In past civil wars, victory has usually been determined by the capture of the country's capital. In a civil war in a nuclear weapon state, victory could be determined by control of the nuclear force. It is possible that some of the nuclear arms would fall to both sides and that this would deter their use. However, when such mutual deterrence does not exist, the temptation for a side losing the conventional battle in a civil war to employ nuclear weapons would be very great indeed. In a bitter civil war of the type waged in Russia in the 1920s, in Spain in the 1930s, in China in the 1940s and in Kampuchea in the 1960s and 1970s, nothing can assure victory but the obliteration of the opposing forces.[37] In these circumstances defeat means the destruction of whole social classes, hence the desperation and brutality with which civil wars are fought. The existence of nuclear weapons in a state riven by this sort of conflict would be a danger to that state as well as to its neighbours. Similarly, in a state divided by civil conflict, such as Iran in 1979, the danger of nuclear weapons falling into the hands of international terrorist organisations would be considerable. Of course, all states may fall prey to civil conflict, but any growth in the number of nuclear weapons increases the danger that they will be used in a civil war and some states *are* more likely to be subject to this sort of internal disorder than others.

Apart from the intrinsic desirability or undesirability of nuclear proliferation, the issue plays an increasingly important part in the North-South debate on security. In nuclear proliferation the developing states have discovered something which the aligned states wish to prevent and in which the developing countries are no longer *demandeurs*. It was therefore the central issue at the May 1978 UN Special Session of Disarmament.[38] The threat to proliferate is sometimes difficult to implement in the present state of the spread of nuclear technology and the more it is used the more the nuclear supplier nations will try to increase their control over the sale of nuclear material. Moreover, no bargaining counter can be used to achieve the impossible. If the Third World uses the threat of nuclear proliferation to try to force the NWS to destroy all their nuclear warheads it will fail because of the intensity of East-West political suspicions and the insurmountable problems of verification. If it uses the threat to achieve more limited goals, such as a cut-off in the production of fissile material for nuclear weapons, further rounds in the SAL negotiations or a comprehensive test ban (CTBT), it may push the negotiations forward, provided the political situation does not deteriorate further and that some of the underlying technical problems, such as verification, can be overcome.

Notes

1. See K. Subrahmanyam, "India's Nuclear Policy", in *Nuclear Proliferation and the Near-Nuclear Countries*, Onkar Marwah and Ann Schulz (eds.), Ballinger, Cambridge, Mass., 1975, p. 125 passim.
2. *Non-Aligned Working Document Containing the Draft Declaration, Programme of Action and Machinery for Implementation,* A/AC 187/55/Add 1, 24 January 1978. This was a revised version of a paper originally submitted to the UN on 18 May 1977.
3. 665 meeting of the UN First Committee, 13 November 1953. See also J.P. Jain, *India and Disarmament Vol 1: The Nehru Era*, Radiant Publishers, New Delhi, 1974.
4. 'Disarmament, Development and a Just World Order, International Workshop on Disarmament', New Delhi, 27-31 March 1978.
5. Ibid.
6. H.G. Pant in *Political Science Review*, January/December 1974, p. 327 passim.
7. 663 meeting of the UN First Committee, 12 November 1953.
8. G.H. Jansen, *Afro-Asia and Non-Alignment*, Faber & Faber, London, 1966, p. 213.
9. 1095 meeting of the UN First Committee, 28 October 1960.
10. 1049 meeting of the UN First Committee, 10 November 1959. See also 1044 meeting, 5 November 1959.
11. See for example the Soviet statement at 686 meeting of the UN First Committee, 11 October 1954.
12. Soviet attitudes are summarised in *Memorandum on Questions Concerning the Ending of the Arms Race and Disarmament*, reproduced in *Soviet News*, London, 19 October 1976.
13. Ibid.
14. See Notes 1 and 4 supra.
15. Klaus Knorr, 'On the international uses of military force in the contem-

porary world', *Orbis*, spring 1977. For the Third World point of view see Jayantanuja Bandyopadhyaya, 'The non-aligned movement in international relations', *India Quarterly*, April-June 1977.

16. Final Document of the UN Special Session on Disarmament, June 1978, para 11. This is reproduced in *United Nations No 1 (1978)*, Cmnd 7267, HMSO, London.

17. S.D. Muni in M. Ayoob (ed.), *Conflict and Intervention in the Third World*, Croom Helm, London, 1980, p. 56.

18. Hedley Bull, 'Arms control and international order', *International Security*, summer 1976. See also the exchange between Alan de Rusett and A. Appadorai in K.P. Misra (ed.), *Foreign Policy of India*, Thomson Press, New Delhi, 1977, p. 97 passim.

19. P.V.R. Rao, *Defence Without Drift*, Bombay Popular Prakashan, 1970, p. 305.

20. Cmd 9075.

21. M. Howard, *Studies in War and Peace*, Viking Press, New York, p. 15. See also Hedley Bull, *The Anarchical Society*, Macmillan, London, 1981, pp. 234-8.

22. 658 meeting of the UN First Committee, 685 and 686 meeting, 11 October 1954 and 808 meeting, 9 December 1955.

23. *Documents on Disarmament 1961*, ACDA, Washington, 1962, p. 355.

24. 1102 meeting of the UN First Committee, 10 November 1961,and 1194 meeting, 14 November 1961.

25. *Documents on Disarmament 1964*, ACDA, Washington, 1965, p. 448.

26. See, for example, K.R. Singh, *The Indian Ocean Big Power Rivalry and Local Response*, Manohar, New Delhi, 1977, p. 245.

27. *UN General Assembly Special Session on Disarmament, Report of the Australian Delegation*, Australian Government Printing Service, 1978, p. 13.

28. 'Leonid Brezhnev's message',*Soviet News*, 22 June 1982.

29. 660 meeting of the UN First Committee, 9 November 1953.

30. 956 meeting of the UN First Committee, 21 October 1958.

31. 804 meeting of the UN First Committee, 6 December 1955. See also the US statement at the 802 meeting, 5 December 1955.

32. See Chapters 10 and 11 below.

33. 'Carter urges a fresh faith', *The Age*, Melbourne, 21 January 1977.

34. 1366 meeting of the UN First Committee, 27 October 1965.

35. See the reprint of the Reith lecture by Ali Mazrui in *Survival*, March/April 1980.

36. For the purported Soviet threats against China see 'Haldeman, Russia urged China A-raid' and 'Tass calls alleged bid to bomb China a lie', *International Herald Tribune*, 18 and 20 February 1978.

37. This can involve merely the expulsion of the losing side as the Vietnamese government showed.

38. P. Towle, 'The UN Special Session on Disarmament – retrospect', *The World Today*, May 1979.

9 ARMS CONTROL AND DEMOCRACY

Governments and Public Opinion

It is ironic and unfortunate that popular interest in arms control and disarmament increases as the international atmosphere darkens and the prospect for negotiating agreements declines. For most of the time press and public interest is muted. Hard-bitten journalists take a cynical attitude towards the question and the amount of Western press coverage of the negotiations is minute. In good times the public in general hardly considers strategic issues at all whilst, in electoral terms, the state of the economy is always likely to be much more important.

These vacillating or cynical attitudes contrast sharply with the behaviour of democratic governments. In good times and bad they generally struggle to achieve arms control and other agreements with potential enemies. They may strive more fervently if they believe the force of public opinion is behind them but strive they will. Since the end of the First World War, there has hardly been a year in which disarmament and arms control negotiations have not been proceeding. Of course, it takes two or more nations to negotiate and totalitarian governments have been involved as well. But it is notable that totalitarian governments do not negotiate arms control agreements amongst themselves, even when they are locked in confrontation. Thus, the Russians and Germans did not do so in the 1930s, nor have the Soviets and Chinese even attempted to do so, despite more than two decades of antagonism and violent confrontation. If this experience is any guide, a world of totalitarian states would be devoid of arms control negotiations. To put it another way, such negotiations are a product of the democratic states' style of diplomacy and of their need to maintain a consensus — to prove to their people that there is no alternative to their current security policies. In part their attitudes can also be explained by simple economics, though it should be noted that economic pressures have not driven the Russians and Chinese to negotiate. But in democracies the defence budget is always under pressure in peacetime and governments hope that a successful agreement might relieve this. Furthermore, democratic foreign ministries have an instinctive belief that an agreement with a potential enemy would be a symbol of improving relations and, whilst cynics may rightly mock the idea of

restraining revisionist states by 'paper treaties', democratic governments feel the need to supplement their defence policies. In the nuclear
age, in particular, statesmen have to show that they have tried every
method of reducing the threat of general war.

Arms control is the foreign policy of defence. However much they
may wish to avoid it by deterrence or other means, defence ministries
have to prepare for the breakdown of international order. Foreign
ministries can help in this process by improving contacts with potential
allies and driving wedges between potential enemies. But their first
instinct is generally to avoid war altogether by improving relations with
threatening states through arms control and other agreements. If war
still occurs, these efforts usually appear misguided or naive, as the
British policy of appeasement appeared in 1939 or British efforts to
settle the Falklands dispute by negotiation with Argentina seemed in
April 1982. On the other hand, a democratic public will only enter a
war united if it is assured that the government has exhausted all hopes
of negotiations.

In such negotiations the open debate and the pressure of an aroused
public opinion in favour of concessions can undoubtedly weaken the
bargaining position of democratic governments. The 'arms control', as
opposed to the 'disarmament' lobby, generally appreciates this point.
This group often accepts that satisfactory agreements can only be
reached by hard bargaining and that it is all too easy for democratic
governments to appear so determined to achieve an agreement that a
potential enemy simply has to wait for concessions to be made. In part
this appears to have been Hitler's tactic *vis-à-vis* the democracies in the
1930s. The desire for flexibility also helps to explain the official dislike
for massive public pressure in favour of concessions in arms control and
other negotiations. Finally, because pressure for disarmament increases
at moments of crisis, when fear of a potential enemy is growing, this
helps to explain the intense hostility of those who distrust the disarmament lobby and accuse it of favouring the country's enemies.[1] Such
accusations are intensely resented; as one of those involved in the
'peace movements' of the early 1980s put it, 'we are a becoming a little
tired of accusations of fellow-travelling, lunacy and naivity emanating
from the Ministry of Defence'.[2]

In one essential respect the problem has increased since 1945. In the
pre-1914 period and again in the 1930s few in the various 'peace movements' could be accused of having ideological sympathy with the
potential enemy — Germany. Many believed that Germany had a right

to a 'place in the sun' before the First World War, hence the efforts of the British Liberal government to persuade Germany to take over the Portuguese colonies should Portugal collapse.[3] Subsequent to the First World War, many argued that Germany had been badly treated at the Versailles conference. As Professor Gilbert Murray put it, 'the Treaty of Versailles, and more particularly, the means of its application, constituted when taken together a gross and crying injustice'.[4] But few actually liked Germany for its own sake – particularly after the rise of Hitler. Today, however, members of the 'peace movement' do argue that the Soviet Union and the West should be put on the same moral level. Thus, one of the movement's leaders told a Czech dissident that the East Europeans

> had constructed in their minds a wholly illusory view of the 'other world' made up of the Voice of America . . . No doubt the reports of less partial observers do not reach you . . . If they should get through you will find a picture more complex than that of a 'free world' here and a 'totalitarian' world there.[5]

Not surprisingly the change from the attitudes of the 1930s accentuates the bitterness of the current debate – a bitterness which is in any case increased by the fear of nuclear as opposed merely to conventional war.

It is natural that the disarmament lobby should ask its own government to make concessions. It is on this government alone that it can bring direct political pressure through elections, demonstrations and the press. Thus, ardent advocates of disarmament will want their own government to 'show others how to behave'. One underlying argument is that, if a nation can cause an arms race by increasing its armaments, then it should be able to stop such a race by reducing its own forces. The spiral should work both ways. The misunderstanding arises from the belief that the government caused the arms race, rather than the political competition and tension with another state. Thus, military gestures alone will not solve a political conflict. Moreover, country A might reduce its armaments but countries B and D might continue to rearm, either because they fear each other or because they intend to dominate country A or to wrest political concessions from it.

The Reaction of Other States

How foreign governments sometimes view unilateralist pressures in a democracy is illustrated by the reports from the German ambassador in Britain before the First World War. Lichnowsky was an Anglophile who fought hard to prevent Britain and Germany drifting into opposite and irreconcilable camps. But he never took the arguments of the British 'peace movement' seriously, though he regarded it as a potent political force. Consequently, if ministers in the Liberal government offered to come to an accommodation with Germany, Lichnowsky argued that their initiatives were merely intended for political and electoral advantage and were not intended to be taken at face value.

Reporting on the Naval Estimates presented by Winston Churchill as First Lord of the Admiralty in March 1913, Lichnowsky stated, 'in the radical newspapers, the pacifists and enthusiasts for disarmament lament even this small increase of expenditure on marine armaments'.[6] In his defence of the Estimates before Parliament two weeks later, Churchill proposed a one-year holiday with Germany in the construction of battleships. On the other hand, he said that, if Germany built more ships than it already planned, Britain would be compelled by its strategic position to build twice as many. Lichnowsky interpreted this arms control proposal solely in tactical terms. Churchill, he argued

> was in a difficult position in so far as in the Left Wing of his own party there is a strong inclination to limit naval armaments, while the Opposition for the most part energetically advocates an extensive building programme . . . The proposal to have a naval holiday after coming to an understanding with Germany was . . . merely made for show and will hardly be taken seriously by anyone here, least of all by Mr Churchill himself.[7]

But it was not long before the ambassador had to eat his words. When he met Churchill at a dinner, the First Lord told him that his proposal was to be taken seriously. Thus, Lichnowsky now concluded that Churchill's motives were technical. 'He seems . . . to attach very great importance, probably on technical and other grounds, to having a pause in naval shipbuilding'. But this did not make the German ambassador suggest that his own government should take Churchill's proposal seriously. Instead he commented,

> as he [Churchill] is very vain, and is bent, come what may, on playing a brilliant part, it will be necessary for us to humour his vanity and to avoid doing anything that might make him look ridiculous, even though the actual result of his suggestions, as I

anticipate, should not correspond with what he hopes for from the plan put forward by him.[8]

Accordingly the German ambassador advised his government to give a 'friendly but evasive answer to any suggestion, putting forward perhaps technical and other difficulties'.[9] Six months later Lichnowsky noted that 'the resistance of the Radical Wing of the government party to the increased British naval expenditure is beginning to cause the government serious difficulties'.[10] At the beginning of 1914 these political problems were increased by Lloyd George's calls for reductions in military expenditure. These, Lichnowsky concluded,

> will bring the radical wing, led by the Chancellor of the Exchequer [Lloyd George] into even more marked opposition to Mr Winston Churchill and his followers . . . That the Radical Left has resolved, come what may, to put a stop to the heavy expenditure of the Minister for the Navy is also proved by a letter published in several papers yesterday by Sir John Brunner, the Chairman of the National Liberal Federation.[11]

When there was talk of Churchill visiting Germany with the British Fleet, Lichnowsky said 'I could perhaps give him to understand that it would be better for him not to refer to the naval holiday or other nonsense of that kind'.[12]

It is clear from Lichnowsky's despatches that political pressure on Churchill by the radical wing of his party helped to make the German ambassador dismiss his proposals. Some may argue, of course, that without this pressure Churchill would never have taken his initiatives, but this is not necessarily so. As he explained to the German ambassador, he believed that 'armaments had gradually become too large and too costly and no State could in the long run stand the strain . . . It would be better to spend the money on more useful things'.[13] There is no reason to doubt the sincerity of these remarks. Churchill had joined the Liberals as a radical and was committed to a radical social programme.

As far as the British government's own anti-military convictions and its reaction to the disarmament lobby goes, some historians have argued that they actually encouraged the Germans to compete with Britain because they gave Germany the possibility that it might catch up or even overtake the navy of its putative enemy. Thus, the historian, R.C.K. Ensor, wrote in 1936, that the construction of the first modern battleship, *Dreadnought*, in 1906 gave Britain a commanding lead in naval strength and, if it had been followed up,

> before such a hopeless handicap . . . the chance of inducing Germany to renounce the race seemed a fairly good one; and it was probably the only alternative, in the light of what we now know, to the solution of war. But . . . it completely disappeared when the Campbell-Bannerman government in 1906-8 by abandoning the Cawdor programme, threw away most of the lead which the genius of [Admiral Sir John] Fisher had secured for Great Britain and encouraged Germany to try drawing level again.[14]

Ensor undoubtedly underestimated the political motivation for the German programme and the strategic desire to persuade Britain to remain neutral out of fear of the German navy in the event of a European war. Moreover, war came in 1914 not because of the Anglo-German naval race but because of the political weakness of Austria-Hungary and its determination to crush Serbia and the determination of the entente to prevent this. Thus, even if the Germans had abandoned their attempt to compete with Britain in naval armaments, the First World War would still have taken place. Nevertheless, Ensor was correct to point out that it was not enough to want to avoid war and military competition with Germany. Governments have to reduce the basic political antagonisms, and British efforts to ignore that problem and to appease Germany militarily may actually have encouraged German competition.

There is no reason to believe that the disarmament lobby was any more acute in its strategic thinking between the two world wars. Hitler and Mussolini regarded it with contempt and it confirmed their impressions that the democracies were too cowardly to fight. Similarly it is difficult to imagine the man who was responsible for the deaths of millions of his fellow Russians, regarding it with any greater sympathy.[15] The question is whether Soviet attitudes have changed since the death of Stalin. For, since 1945, attitudes towards disarmament and arms control in the West have been determined largely by two factors — assessment of the likelihood of nuclear war and fear of the Soviet Union. Some may object that these two fears are synonymous but this is not so and they often have quite different effects on attitudes towards arms control and disarmament. The more people fear that there is a danger of war breaking out, the more they are likely to favour arms control and disarmament measures which they believe may reduce that danger. On the other hand, the more people fear the Soviet Union and distrust its intentions, the less likely they are to believe that effective arms control measures can be negotiated with the Soviet leaders.

Of course the two factors may interact. A deep-seated belief that nuclear war is likely to occur sometimes makes commentators more optimistic about the Soviet Union's political ambitions because they are so concerned to see East-West arms control measures negotiated. Conversely, those who greatly distrust Soviet intentions may play down the danger of nuclear war and the possibility of achieving any worthwhile arms control measures with the East. Evidently, there are those who are pessimistic both about the dangers of nuclear war and about Soviet intentions and this attitude was predominant in the West during the Cold War of the 1950s. But, wherever an analyst places himself upon the two axes, there can be no doubt about their importance in determining attitudes towards disarmament and arms control.

Attitudes Towards the Soviet Union

Those who admire the Soviet state and have great faith in its intentions frequently become advocates of unilateral Western disarmament. As the author of a letter to the *Guardian* put it,

> I do not believe that the Soviet Union would treat unilateral disarmament by Britain or phased disarmament by the West as a sign of weakness to be exploited, but rather as a positive move to defuse a dangerous situation.[16]

Generally such commentators argue that Soviet armaments are the result either of bitter historical experience of invasions from Napoleon to Hitler or of the reaction to Western armaments. According to a letter in *The Times*,

> the numerous attempts by the Russians to establish disarmament talks and to wind down confrontation in Europe are a matter of historical record . . . We stand a good chance of total annihilation as the consequence of an American attack on the Soviet Union which, by their own calculations, would leave the USA unscathed.[17]

Some might argue that, if there were no Soviet 'threat' there would be no point in the disarmament negotiations since these only take place between potentially hostile powers. But here the other factor − fear of nuclear war − comes into play. Some believe that wars may break out, as the author of the letter in *The Times* quoted above argued, because of Western aggression. Alternatively they may result from misunderstandings between the Soviet Union and the West or between China and the Soviet Union, or even from the technical failure of one of the nuclear forces. Unilateral Western reductions would reduce the prospects for Western expansionism and encourage the (benevolent) Russians to reduce their forces. If war were then still to take place through a technical error, the damage caused would be reduced.

Moving to the right of the pro-Soviet group, one finds those who by no means necessarily admire the Soviet Union but who believe that its expansionist tendencies have been exaggerated in the West.[18] In 1979 George Kennan accused his critics of contending,

> that the nature of Soviet institutions and internal practices constitutes an effective bar to the achievement of an acceptable *modus vivendi* with that power in the politico-military field . . . that the outcome of the problems of the relationship can be determined only by relentless military competition, to which no end would be conceivable other than some military-political showdown.[19]

Furthermore, Kennan argued that the existence of nuclear weapons presented 'a greater danger than any of the political issues involved in the East-West relationship'. Thus, like the first group who have a high degree of trust in Soviet intentions, this sector also usually strongly supports arms control measures, such as SALT, 'to bring under some sort of control the insane, expensive and dangerous competition in the development of nuclear and other weaponry'.[20] Nevertheless, this group is often less attracted by the idea of unilateral disarmament than those to the left. Its members are often part of the arms control rather than disarmament lobby. Both groups were, however, disappointed by the decline of detente. This disappointment and the general frustration of expectations helped to give rise to the 'peace movement' of the 1980s.

At the other end of this axis are those with very little faith in Soviet intentions. One might expect that those who believe the Russians are expansionist should also believe that there is a high danger of nuclear war. But this is not necessarily so. For those who believe that the Russians take a ruthless approach to the world scene may also believe that they can be deterred by the threat of war. Suspicions of Soviet intentions are partly a reflection of its capabilities. As one commentator has put it,

> it is possible to assert as a general proposition that Soviet military strength is entirely disproportionate to any possible requirement for the territorial defence of the Soviet Union . . . More specifically, any careful examination of the equipment, deployment and tactical doctrines and training methods of the Soviet armed forces seems clearly to establish an aggressive intent.[21]

Many believe that the Russians only advocate disarmament measures in order to lower Western resistance or to trick Western governments into one-sided reductions in their forces. Furthermore, they frequently believe that the Kremlin would cheat on any agreements in order to establish and then to use its superiority. As a US official told the UN in 1954, 'it has been well known for some time that we in the United States suspect the Soviet Union of planning world conquest behind its façade of disarmament statements'.[22]

Fear of Nuclear War

If one looks at the other factor affecting attitudes towards disarmament, one finds the same sweep of opinion. On the one side are those with a very pessimistic attitude towards nuclear war. Their attitudes were perhaps best summarised by Bertrand Russell when he claimed that 'it is absolutely necessary if mankind is to survive that the hydrogen bomb should be banned everywhere'.[23] Into this group falls the Pugwash movement, which Russell helped to found, and which is symbolised by the clock with its fingers approaching midnight. Owing to their intense fear of nuclear war, some of the members of this group may trust the Soviet Union because they are afraid that suspicion may delay disarmament measures and increase the possibility that war may break out. Thus, one of the leading members of the Pugwash movement, Bernard Feld, has criticised those 'whose sensibilities have been . . . irreparably dulled by the cries of "Soviet wolf" from the Neanderthal right'.[24]

Of course, there are also commentators who have a high estimate of the probability of nuclear war and who fear the Soviet Union. These are often extremely sensitive to the charge that they are pro-Soviet if they support disarmament measures. Theirs is in fact the most difficult position because they see both the desirability of improving relations with the Soviet Union in principle and the difficulty of achieving it in practice. This combination of intense fear of nuclear war and of Soviet intentions was most prevalent during the Cold War. Indeed, it is fair to say that many members of the British government in the 1950s fell into this category. Harold Macmillan recorded in his memoirs that, when he visited the Prime Minister, Winston Churchill, in 1954, he found him 'still brooding about the atomic and hydrogen bombs and the terrible destructive power that seemed to menace the future of mankind'.[25] Similarly, Churchill's doctor, Lord Moran, wrote, 'in his heart [Churchill] has a great fear; he dreads another war because he does not believe that England would survive'.[26]

As a result of their fear of nuclear war, Churchill and Macmillan were strong advocates of arms control measures. Commentators are fond of saying that the negotiators involved in the arms control and disarmament conferences of the 1950s were more concerned with making political points than with achieving agreements. But this was not so. In Macmillan's view,

> Churchill was obsessed by his hopes of going down to history not only as the greatest War Minister but as the greatest peacemaker in the world. He was, therefore, thinking only of Russia.[27]

When he had a stroke in June 1953 Churchill told Moran that it prevented him from bringing the Russians and the Americans together; 'I feel . . . I could do something that no one else can do . . . not perhaps world peace but world easement. I feel I could have changed the bias of the world'.[28] Macmillan's revelation in his memoirs that he wept with relief when he heard that the Partial Test Ban Treaty had been signed, hardly supports the image sometimes presented of the leaders of that period being indifferent to arms control.[29] Their problem was that their fear of nuclear war encouraged them to negotiate with the Russians but their suspicions of Soviet intentions, together with Soviet obstruction, prevented most of the negotiations reaching any far-reaching agreement.

In the 1960s and 1970s the fear both of the danger of nuclear war and of Soviet intentions declined considerably. There were, however, still commentators who pointed to the dangers from both. Lord Chalfont is interesting in this respect. He has argued that the 'arms race

. . . in the long run can only end in a disastrous conflagration' and deplored 'the insanity of a world so organized that it spends such ingenuity and such treasure on the pursuit of mutual blackmail'. But, at the same time, he has attacked 'the agents of our enemies [who] have long sought to deny the existence of a "Soviet threat" '. Whilst he has supported certain arms control agreements, he has warned that 'spectacular agreements on nuclear disarmament are simply not available' and that 'we dare not give anything away while the Soviet military build-up goes on'.[30]

On the other end of this axis are those with a very low fear of nuclear war breaking out. This may be because they believe that the Soviet Union is not expansionist or because they believe that the Super Powers have been taught moderation by having to learn to live with the threat of nuclear war. As Anthony Hartley has pointed out:

> it was a basic characteristic of the era of deterrence that countries possessed of, and faced by, nuclear weapons would do their utmost to avoid placing themselves or others in situations where vital issues were raised without any line of retreat on either side. The concomitant of nuclear deterrence was political prudence.[31]

Those with a very low fear of the threat of nuclear war are unlikely to give strong support to arms control measures to lower still further the risk of such a catastrophe, although they may not be hostile to balanced disarmament measures and may support such agreements in order to reduce defence budgets and to allow greater expenditure on more 'socially useful' projects.

On the whole, Western governments are necessarily more concerned with assessing the Soviet threat than with trying to decide the probability of the occurrence of nuclear war. Assessment of Soviet intentions is difficult and many Western analyses have been mistaken but it is at least possible to discuss these intentions rationally. Conclusions can be based on an examination of the data, such as previous Soviet actions, the speeches of Soviet leaders, the level of Soviet armaments and the direction of their military strategies. Attempts to assess the chances of a major East-West war breaking out are much more hazardous. According to Professor Rapoport;

> Nor can the so-called 'probability' of a nuclear war be meaningfully estimated. Probabilities of events are estimated from the frequencies of their occurrence. Thus, it makes sense to speak of the probability

of an air crash, a fire, a tornado, but not of a nuclear war, unless such wars become recurring events.[32]

Nevertheless, however imprecise such estimates may be, it is clear that the desire to reduce the chances of nuclear war has influenced policy in the arms control area. In June 1963 the United States and the Soviet Union established a direct communications link 'to reduce the danger that accident, miscalculation or surprise attack might trigger a nuclear war'.[33] Of course, some analysts are rightly very sceptical of the idea that wars are caused by such miscalculations. As Evan Luard has argued,

> it remains to be shown that, even under the conditions of modern armaments systems, misunderstandings and miscalculations are ever themselves the cause of war . . . The outbreak of hostilities has not been the effect of accident or miscalculation as normally understood. It has been deliberate and calculated.[34]

Whether this is true or not, and I believe that it is, the USA and Soviet Union have worked since 1963 to improve the communications link and to reduce the prospects for inadvertent war. As a result of their efforts, an agreement on measures to reduce the risk of the outbreak of nuclear war was signed in September 1971. Both Super Powers pledged to maintain and to improve measures for preventing accidental or unauthorised use of nuclear weapons. They also agreed to 'arrangements for immediate notification should a risk of nuclear war arise from such incidents from detection of unidentified objects on early warning systems'. They also agreed to give advance warning of any missile launch beyond their own territory and in the direction of the other party.[35]

However, it was not such specific measures but the whole climate of detente which reduced general Western fears of nuclear war in the 1960s and 1970s. As the international atmosphere worsened again at the beginning of the 1980s public fears began again to increase. Some of the confidence which had been built up by the earlier agreements was also dissipated by reports that computer errors had caused US forces to be put on alert three times in seven months. The first of these reports in November 1979 said that ten jet interceptors from bases in the United States and Canada had taken off because of a false computer report that the country was under attack by a number of Soviet missiles.[36] Further reports in June 1980 suggested that US forces had been put on alert twice in a matter of days.[37] Whilst none of these alerts appear to have been very serious, they undoubtedly increased public pessimism about the chances of nuclear war breaking out by mistake.

Soviet and Chinese Views

The Soviet leaders have tried to increase Western fears of the dangers of nuclear war and to reduce suspicions of their own intentions. By doing so they hope to increase the likelihood of the West agreeing to the disarmament proposals which they advance. Thus, the communist press presents Soviet armaments as limited in scale and as purely a response to the Western build-up: 'Leonid Brezhnev has stressed that the Soviet Union is not seeking for military superiority. The Soviet Union considers that a rough balance and parity are sufficient for the needs of defence'.[38] Soviet commentators argue that the USSR has never attacked another country and that the military actions against Finland and Poland before the Soviet Union entered the Second World War and against Hungary, Czechoslovakia and Afghanistan subsequently were purely defensive. 'The world at large is well aware that the Soviet Union has never threatened anyone with war or attacked anyone. This is forcefully illustrated by the more than 60 years of the existence of the Soviet state'.[39] Consequently, as Mr Gromyko told the UN General Assembly in 1979, 'anyone who trusts [Soviet] policy will never be let down. The USSR and the socialist countries can always be relied upon in the struggle for peace, disarmament and detente'.[40]

The Chinese have responded to Soviet claims in recent years by outlining a very different view of the world situation. They have argued that the outbreak of a nuclear war is likely, although they have dismissed its effects. They have also likened Soviet policy to Hitler's policy before 1939. Thus, Mr Huang told the UN First Committee in November 1976,

as Chairman Mao Tsetung has pointed out, the current international situation is characterized by great disorder under heaven and it is excellent . . . The international situation has grown more tense. It can be seen clearly that in the present world the factors for both revolution and war are visibly increasing.[41]

Mr Huang went on to claim that, while it was applauding detente, the

Soviet Union has not shown any restraint in its wild ambitions, but has become ever more rampant. It has kept on stepping up its military threat and political subversion against Western Europe.

The Chinese leadership claims, therefore, to have a low fear of the effects of nuclear war and a high level of distrust of the Soviet Union. The result is that it is very sceptical of arms control measures and has not signed any of the treaties negotiated in recent years. Admittedly China has become more involved in international discussions on disarmament since the death of Mao Tsetung but it is evidently more interested in building up its forces to balance the Soviet Union than in any sort of agreement which might preserve the Super Powers' military dominance. As China informed the UN Secretary General in April 1979, 'when major progress has been made in the reduction of the armaments of the Super Powers, other nuclear countries will join them in reducing their armaments in a reasonable ratio . . . The crux of the matter lies in the lack of sincerity of the Super Powers, which have always tried to cover up their arms expansion by empty talk'.[42]

The public position of the non-aligned countries is precisely the opposite of the Chinese. The non-aligned claim that they have a high fear of the danger of nuclear war and rarely admit to fear of Soviet expansionism. According to the Bureau of the non-aligned nations, 'the hazards and perils of the arms race to the maintenance of international peace and security and the development and survival of mankind necessitate a serious effort to halt and eventually eliminate this race'.[43] Because the non-aligned argue that the United States and the Soviet Union are equally menacing, they frequently contend that Western demands for verification and for the preservation of the military balance in agreements are merely devices to hinder the progress of nuclear disarmament. They regard almost any East-West disarmament measure as beneficial and constantly criticise the lack of progress towards general and complete disarmament.

Conclusion

Fear of war and fear of the Soviet Union are not, of course, the only factors which determine Western attitudes towards disarmament and arms control. There are also deep divisions between those who believe with Anthony Hartley that 'disarmament, after all, is the consequence of a measure of political agreement rather than its cause',[44] and those, such as Lord Brockway and Noel Baker, who believe that the deterioration in the international situation 'provides a unique opportunity for worldwide pressure by people to end the danger of a nuclear war which threatens to· destroy the greater part of the earth's population'.[45] In a tense atmosphere the gaps between such opinions are likely to widen. What does this mean for the long-term prospects for arms control? If the international atmosphere lightened once again and both the fears of Soviet intentions and of nuclear war declined, then public demonstrations would be less of a driving force behind the Western negotiators. On the other hand, governments could make greater concessions because the degree of trust would be higher. Conversely, if we entered a new Cold War, the fervour of those groups demanding disarmament would increase. Thus, such periods of tension are characterised in the West by political disunity and by far-reaching disarmament proposals. But the negotiations are blocked by growing fear of the Soviet Union. Aspirin is not an appropriate treatment for cancer. Thus, the periods of detente offer better prospects both of achieving an internal political consensus and of negotiating arms control agreements – a point nicely illustrated by the first two UN Special Sessions devoted to disarmament. *The Times* commented after the 1982 session, 'the most striking irony about the failure of the session was that it met at a time of intense public awareness and activity, where members of the public had remained generally oblivious of the first session [in 1978] which had been termed a success.'[46]

Notes

1. The Earl of Kimberley, quoted in *The Times*, 26 November 1981.
2. *Guardian*, 21 September 1981.
3. A.J. Grant and H. Temperley, *Europe in the Nineteenth and Twentieth Centuries*, Longmans Green, London, 1973, p. 480.
4. Gilbert Murray, *The Intelligent Man's Way to Prevent War*, Gollancz, London, 1933, p. 69. See also Hampden Jackson, *The Post War World*, Gollancz, London, 1935, p. 50.
5. 'Freedom and the Bomb', *New Statesman*, 24 April 1981.
6. Prince Lichnowsky, *Heading for the Abyss*, Constable, London, 1958, p. 331.
7. Lichnowsky, p. 334.
8. Lichnowsky, p. 335.
9. Lichnowsky, p. 336.
10. Lichnowsky, p. 340.
11. Lichnowsky, p. 342.
12. Lichnowsky, p. 347.
13. Lichnowsky, p. 336.
14. R.C.K. Ensor, *England 1870-1914*, Clarendon Press, Oxford, 1936, p. 364.

15. R. Conquest, *The Great Terror*, Pelican, Harmondsworth, 1971.
16. Letter to the *Guardian*, 17 October 1981.
17. Letter to *The Times*, 11 July 1981.
18. Letter to *The Times* 28 October 1981.
19. G.F. Kennan, 'A last warning', *Encounter*, July 1978.
20. Ibid.
21. Alun Chalfont, 'Arguing about war and peace', *Encounter*, January 1981.
22. 693 meeting of the UN First Committee, 19 October 1954.
23. Quoted in A.J.R. Groom, *British Thinking about Nuclear Weapons*, Francis Pinter, London, 1975, p. 573.
24. B.T. Feld, 'Disaster through the back door', *Bulletin of the Atomic Scientists*, May 1974. The Stockholm International Peace Research Institute (SIPRI) falls to a great extent into this category. See F. Barnaby, *Nuclear Disarmament or Nuclear War?*, SIPRI, Stockholm, 1975, p. 27.
25. H. Macmillan, *Tides of Fortune, 1945-1955*, Macmillan, London, 1969, p. 530.
26. Lord Moran, *Winston Churchill, the Struggle for Survival*, Constable, London, 1966, p. 503 passim.
27. Macmillan, *Tides of Fortune*, p. 533.
28. Moran, *Winston Churchill*, p. 410.
29. H. Macmillan, *At the End of the Day, 1961-1963*, Macmillan, London, 1973, p. 487.
30. Lord Chalfont, 'Sharing responsibility for what Mr Carter signs in Moscow', *The Times*, 15 February 1977; 'As the arms balance tilts against the West "doom watching" is less of a joke', *The Times*, 6 September 1977. See also loc. cit., 4 April 1977.
31. Anthony Hartley, 'Balancing the bomb, the dilemma of nuclear weapons', *Encounter*, December 1980, p. 82.
32. A. Rapoport (ed.), *Clausewitz on War*, Penguin, Harmondsworth, 1968, p. 51.
33. *Arms Control and Disarmament Agreements*, ACDA, Washington, 1977, p. 27 passim.
34. E. Luard, *Conflict and Peace in the Modern International System*, University of London Press, 1970, p. 189. See also G. Blainey, *The Causes of War*, Sun Books, Melbourne, 1977, p. 127.
35. ACDA, *Arms Control*, p. 102 passim.
36. 'Top officials not told of alert', *Canberra Times*, 12 November 1979.
37. 'Error puts US on alert', *Canberra Times*, 7 June 1980.
38. *Soviet News*, 11 December 1979, p. 404.
39. Marshal N. Ogarkov, *Soviet News*, 21 August 1979.
40. *Soviet News*, 2 October 1979.
41. Records of the UN First Committee, 8 November 1976, A/c.1./31/PV.25.
42. Chinese reply to the Secretary General, 12 September 1979, A/Cn.10/1, 19 April 1979.
43. Communication dated 18 May 1977 from the Chairman of the Coordinating Bureau of the Non-Aligned countries to the UN Secretary General.
44. Hartley, 'Balancing the bomb', p. 84.
45. Letter to *The Times*, 2 January 1981.
46. 'Bitterness at failure of UN arms control', *The Times*, 12 July 1982.

Part Three

ARMS CONTROL

10 VERIFICATION – HISTORY

Introduction

We have then the democratic electorates which take a spasmodic interest in arms control and disarmament, led by statesmen and diplomats who methodically plod away at the problem; a group of communist states which pursue their own strategic interests determinedly and consistently but have a common interest with the democracies in avoiding nuclear war; and we have a large group of Third World countries which act as the chorus to the negotiations. These take a generally pro-Soviet view of strategy, though they also have an interest in avoiding nuclear war and in enhancing their relative power. Apart from the clashing political interests of these negotiating blocs, the difficulty of the subject limits what can be achieved. The first great technical problem is verification, which is intimately linked to the root of the security problem, East-West political hostility.

Governments are not inherently truthful. This applies to democratic as well as to totalitarian regimes of the right and left. The first reaction of any government caught out in some nefarious or dubious activity may be to hide the truth. Thus Sir Anthony Eden denied that there was any collusion between the British, French and Israeli governments before the Suez operation in 1956, although there had certainly been conversations between ministers from the three countries.[1] The first reaction of the United States government, after the U2 spy plane had been shot down over the Soviet Union in 1959, was to deny that it had been ordered to overfly Soviet territory – though President Eisenhower subsequently accepted responsibility.[2] Similarly the Kremlin denied that any 'offensive' weapons were being placed in Cuba in October 1962, although the United States was able to show the Security Council photographs of the missiles being assembled on the island.[3] Again in November 1981 the Soviet Union claimed that its Whiskey class submarine, which grounded in a prohibited area off the coast of Sweden, had gone off course because of a failure of its navigational instruments. However, Swedish experts later demonstrated that this was not true, despite continued Soviet denials.[4] If this history shows anything, it is that democratic governments are usually caught out in their falsehoods and very often forced to retract, whilst dictatorships find it easier to maintain their lies.

Given the propensity of governments to act in this way, it is not surprising that they have asked for inspection to be included in arms control agreements which touch on their vital interests. They know the limitations of others because they know their own. Thus, the demand for inspection is as old as the disarmament proposals themselves. On the first occasion in modern times when a government called a general conference to limit armaments — the Hague Peace Conference in 1899 — the problem of verification arose. When the Russians called for disarmament, the British delegate, Sir John Ardagh, asked what there was to stop a state making rifles on an entirely new pattern and storing them in secret 'and whether there would be any inspection of an international character to ensure that the convention was properly adhered to by all signatory states?'[5] The Russians replied that public opinion and parliaments were adequate safeguards, though this response came somewhat oddly from an undemocratic autocracy. Moreover, the question had been tabled and it was never to go away. In 1899 there was no chance that many of the states concerned would agree to any statutory limitations and so the problem of verification was never examined in detail. However, in the 1920s, when disarmament was taken more seriously, the question of inspection arose once more and the conflict that it would create with the principle of sovereignty and the need for national secrecy immediately became apparent.

The Interwar Period

The general attitude of the British and American governments in the 1920s was to oppose any international inspection on their territories, on the grounds that it would infringe their sovereignty. In his instructions to one US delegation attending an international conference, Secretary of State Kellogg laid down 'the United States will not tolerate the supervision of any outside body in this matter nor be subjected to inspection or supervision by foreign agencies or individuals'.[6] Viscount Cecil, the British delegate, suggested that countries should rely on information from their military attachés[7] and thus it was left to the French to emphasise the importance of inspection if confidence were to be created:

> Do you not feel [their delegate asked] that without a system of verification you will have created a state of mistrust and that, in the

absence of detailed information and with a prevailing impression that the Convention is not being scrupulously applied in one quarter or another, other parties will be tempted to embark on the same course?

As one member of the British delegation put it,

the truth was that, much as the French disliked the idea of their own establishments being inspected, they were prepared to swallow all this in order to have similar rights of investigation in Germany.[8]

In public, Anglo-American attitudes appeared to move closer to the French in the 1930s. One US historian has argued that in the American case this was as a result of the growing deterioration in the international climate and of the increasing fear of war. In its briefs for the US delegation to the League disarmament conference in 1932, the Hoover administration argued that an International Supervisory Agency might be acceptable, provided that it was only to 'study and report' on purported breaches in any agreement.[9] By July 1932 Secretary of State Stimson said he was prepared to accept inspection on US territory and this policy was endorsed when the Democratic administration under F.D. Roosevelt took office. The German ambassador in Washington reported in May 1933:

the President said that he would also be willing, if others should do so, to subject America to supervision by an international commission with respect to her state of disarmament, in spite of the misgivings about this within his own administration and in particular by the Hearst press.[10]

The British believed that the changes in the US position had been forced by the pressure of public opinion. As E.H. Carr wrote from the British delegation in Geneva on 23 November 1932,

it is true that we are not entirely isolated on this matter [opposition to intensive inspection] but US delegates are too afraid of their own public opinion to put up an effective opposition against the proposals for control however little they may like them.[11]

The British government was deeply divided about the whole issue. In July 1932 it agreed to accept inspection following accusations of violations of any agreed treaty, though not to accept general inspections.[12] But this hardly solved the problem. As the Admiralty pointed out,

> it would be impossible, for instance, to prevent the admission of inspectors to the state cordite factory . . . it would be easy for a foreign government to make an allegation that poison gas was being manufactured and thus to secure an inspection.[13]

Brigadier Temperley, one of the serving officers at the League conference in Geneva, pointed out that, if an inspection were refused, it would 'open up an obvious loophole for evasion and may give the impression that we have something to conceal.'[14]

Only too well aware of the problems of concealment, the League committee looking into the question of verification increasingly wanted verification measures to be as wide as possible.[15] There were also suggestions that private individuals should be able to report their government's alleged infringements of agreements to an international body and be immune from prosecution. The Chief of the Imperial General Staff minuted sourly:

> if legal immunity was enacted for the protection of all informers regarding alleged breaches of the disarmament convention, any spy would obtain legal immunity. [But, he added] it will be remembered that during the last few years there have been several cases in which disclosures by Germans of alleged breaches of the Versailles Treaty have been followed by heavy sentences of imprisonment for high treason by German courts.[16]

Thus, the advantages of giving citizens immunity to report the malefactions of their own governments were obvious, but so were the disadvantages. Ironically the dictatorships, such as Japan and Russia, claimed that they would allow their citizens to report on their behaviour, though the British had no faith in their protestations.[17]

In September 1933 the Cabinet decided, somewhat cautiously, that if the only barrier to a convention were the question of supervision, the British government would not regard this as necessarily constituting an insuperable obstacle, but would consider the proposal with an anxious desire of finding a means of supervision acceptable to all.[18]

However, the Cabinet committee looking into the problem was more sceptical. Its concern with security was such that the limitations it would have imposed on inspection would have negated any utility which it might have had. Information should only be given to an international agency if the government were prepared to give such information to Parliament, in other words if it were not secret. It also argued that any subsequent inspection carried out should be on the basis of this information 'and not upon any extraneous matter in the hands of individual members of the Committee'. Furthermore, if there were inspection to ensure that banned weapons were not being hidden, this would open

> up at once unlimited possibilities for the operations of an inspecting body. There are indeed few documents or establishments which might not conceivably contain evidence of the existence of prohibited material.[19]

Surprise inspection visits might be necessary to achieve adequate inspection but these would cause great friction. Thus, the government would want 'to ensure that the proposed items of inspection are relevant to the actual subjects of restriction', making surprise visits impossible. Furthermore, the Cabinet committee believed that,

> the interests of national security would be best served by a provision in the Convention itself that the Parties reserved the right to refuse access to particular documents and establishments, including ships, in cases in which they considered that the interests of security were paramount. [However] the difficulty of proposing the insertion of any such formula in the Convention is obvious.[20]

Thus, on the one hand there were great problems in reconciling inspection with sovereignty and secrecy whilst, on the other, the Cabinet committee believed that there would be awe-inspiring problems for any body trying to ensure that a disarmament convention was being adequately fulfilled. If the number of men in the armed forces was limited, it would be extremely difficult to ensure that numerical totals were not exceeded. If equipment were limited, the numbers of tanks and aircraft could be counted but geographical considerations would render this a slow task and, moreover, a Supervisory Committee could never certify that all the material in commission had been produced for their inspection.

Similarly, if chemical weapon production were banned, it would be relatively easy for a state determined to breach the agreement to use civilian factories for producing such weapons. Moreover, this was true of other equipment and there were 10,000 to 12,000 factories in Britain which were capable of producing armaments of one sort or another. Finally the committee concluded,

> if, in a small and highly-organised country like the United Kingdom, supervision presents considerable practical difficulties, the immensity of the task in countries where, as in the case of Russia or the United States, vast territories would have to be covered, can well be realised.[21]

Whilst the Cabinet committee was deliberating on these matters, it noted that the naval arms control agreements negotiated over the previous decade or more were 'based on good faith, and were drafted with no thought of applying any system of international supervision'. In the Admiralty view they had worked satisfactorily 'and no system of supervision would have been of benefit in ensuring their observance'. Yet the admirals knew at that time that there had been breaches and their attitude must have stemmed from conservatism and reluctance to accept inspection on their own ships and territories. The breaches were partly the result of loose drafting of the original agreements, partly the result of a natural desire to 'bend' the rules as much as possible and partly the result of rank dishonesty. According to Part 3d of the Washington Naval agreement, 'no retained capital ships or aircraft carriers shall be reconstructed except for the purpose of providing means of defence against air and submarine attack'.[22] Yet Britain and the United States modified the bridges and control positions of their capital ships, thereby 'bending' the agreement. The United States went further and increased the effective ranges of its ships' guns from 24,000 to 38,000 yards and it converted two battlecruisers into the aircraft carriers, *Saratoga* and *Lexington*, which each infringed the Treaty limits on aircraft carrier displacement by 3,000 tons. The Italian battle-cruisers of the Littorio class exceeded the Washington limits by 6,000 tons, whilst the Japanese extensively (and secretly) modified the Kongo class of battlecruisers. More importantly they grossly exceeded the limits on aircraft carriers. The *Kaga* exceeded treaty limits by 5,200 tons and *Akaji* by 3,500. Moreover, the Japanese were limited by the agreement to 81,000 tons of aircraft carriers in all, whilst they actually constructed ships displacing 92,770 tons.[23]

Japan's policy seems to have been consistently governed by the desire to persuade potential enemies to underestimate its power. By the late 1930s it was no longer formally bound by international law but, when the British, French and US governments asked the Japanese in 1938 whether they were still abiding by the agreements, they replied that there was no reason to suppose the Treaty limits were being infringed.[24] Yet, Japan was building four high-speed oil tankers and five liners which could be swiftly converted into aircraft carriers when war broke out, although this certainly infringed the spirit of Article XIV of the Washington Treaty. Furthermore, the giant 64,000-ton Yamato class battleships – almost double the size permitted under Article V of the Washington Treaty – were built in great secrecy. High fences were constructed around the shipyards and the harbours were completely cleared when the ships were launched.

If limitations under the Washington Treaty were breached by the parties when they had been voluntarily accepted, so were the limitations *imposed* on Germany by the Treaty of Paris. In the years immediately after the war the victorious Allies had set up an Allied Control Commission to ensure that the Germans were abiding by the disarmament clauses of the treaties. Four hundred officers worked for the Commission under the French General Nollet. From time to time it succeeded in locating hidden weapons including, for example, 600 105 mm gun barrels, but it certainly did not achieve the disarmament of Germany.[25] Its members were sometimes attacked and could not usually visit a factory in sufficient secrecy to ensure surprise and to prevent evasions of the agreements. The great mass of Germans believed that their country had been badly treated by the Allies and were willing to overlook or connive at infringements. Moreover, although the disarmament of Germany was largely a British idea,[26] which was accepted with some scepticism by the French, the British were evidently less determined to enforce it, to the irritation of their allies.

In 1926 the Commission ceased to inspect German territory.[27] It was supposed to be replaced by inspection under the League but the Germans were reluctant to allow this to become effective. As Gustav Stresemann, the German Chancellor, put it in January 1926, the German government,

are prepared to grant to the members of the League Commission every facility. [But] some of the powers contemplated for the League organ of control *vis à vis* the German authorities and private individuals however substantially exceeded what is compatible with the German view.[28]

Thus, effective supervision ceased. But officials in other countries knew that Germany was systematically evading the Treaty long before, particularly through co-operation with the Russians. The Germans tested prohibited weapons, such as chemical agents, on Soviet territory and thus kept abreast, or even ahead, of the prevailing technology. Banned from maintaining an air force, they financed and ran a tactical flying school at Lipetek south east of Moscow.[29] They also produced airliners which could be converted into bombers and which replicated much of the technology involved in the construction of military aircraft. The German Navy helped German companies to establish or buy naval construction facilities in other countries so that they could evade the Treaty limits. Thus, although Germany was not allowed to build submarines, the Navy was able to experiment with vessels under construction for other governments and, when the limitations were finally overtly thrown off, construction of the most modern vessels could rapidly proceed. Even at that stage the British government hoped that agreements might limit the pace of German naval construction, hence the negotiation of the Anglo-German Naval Agreement in 1935. Presumably the Admiralty hoped that the Germans would behave differently towards an agreement they had voluntarily accepted, rather than the one imposed upon them. Yet the voluntary agreement was also systematically breached. Some of the destroyers built in this period exceeded the Treaty limits by as much as one third, whilst the battleship *Bismarck*, launched in 1934, actually displaced 41,700 tons, not 35,000 as the Germans claimed for the purpose of the Anglo-German Agreement.[30]

The Germans were not alone in their infringement of the Versailles Treaty. The Conference of Ambassadors supervising the disarmament of Austria also concluded that Austria had 'not complied with all the requirements demanded of her'.[31] Subsequently they complained that the Austrians imported armoured cars in violation of the agreements, allowed unlawful paramilitary organisations to exist and did not destroy all the armaments factory buildings required. Nevertheless, the Allies concluded that the Austrians did not want war, nor were they capable for the moment of fighting;[32] they soon came to feel differently about Germany.

Discussions since 1945

The failure of many of the international efforts to achieve disarmament, either by agreement or by force, between the two world wars no more deterred statesmen after 1945 from trying to achieve disarmament, than the failure of the League of Nations deterred them from the establishment of the United Nations. Even whilst the war was in progress, the US was planning to negotiate disarmament agreements and to ask for inspection to ensure that they were being observed.[33] The invention of the atomic bomb appeared to make both disarmament and inspection more necessary. If before 1939 a state had infringed a disarmament agreement and hidden part of its tank or air force, this might have made some difference to the outcome of the subsequent war, as German evasion of the Paris agreements in the 1920s helped Hitler achieve his initial victories. But, if after 1945 a state hid some nuclear weapons, as the French representative told the UN in 1955, it would be able: 'to dominate at a chosen time a devastated and radiation-contaminated world or at least to constrain it to accept the worst of ultimatums.'[34]

Western insistence on inspection was also, no doubt, encouraged by the nature of the Soviet state which now gradually became the main potential enemy. Even at the height of the war, when vast quantities of British and US equipment were being shipped to the Soviet Union, no information was supplied to the Allies about Soviet equipment.[35] Thus, faced with a country about whose decision-making process virtually nothing was known and where secrecy had been raised to unprecedented heights, it was not surprising that Western governments wanted inspection to accompany substantial agreements. They were in the position of the French in the 1920s, wanting inspection to monitor the activities of their potential enemies, however reluctant they might have been to see it operate in their own territories.

It was also hardly surprising that the Russians opposed such inspection. Russian society had always been secretive, the communist government vastly accentuated this tendency. The overt Soviet position had been consistent since the 1930s. In September 1933 Maxim Litvinov, the Soviet Foreign Minister, told the German chargé d'affaires in Moscow that his government would only agree to supervision 'after effective disarmament'. Yet the Soviet Union could not have agreed to adequate verification at that time whether or not disarmament had taken place. Had it done so the whole mechanism of the totalitarian state would have been exposed when the Great Terror was beginning.

Moreover, even today, international inspection on any scale would transform the nature of the Soviet state just as effectively as the full implementation of CSCE would. Secrecy and suspicion are the essence of such a political system and this secrecy would plainly be menaced by a large body of international inspectors wandering around the countryside looking for hidden weapons. The Soviet government may have thought that it was politically wise in the 1930s to say that it would accept inspection should disarmament take place. But it is inconceivable that it would have accepted this in practice. Thus, the more the Western nations pushed after 1945 for international inspection, the more it must have seemed to the Russians to be an attempt to subvert their system. The more the Russians opposed such inspection, the more the Western nations began to suspect Soviet intentions. In the Eastern view verification was intended, 'to furnish the United States and its supporters with intelligence information concerning the armed forces and armaments of all countries, such information to be used in preparation for war.'[36] Conversely, the Western position was expressed succinctly by the British representative, Selwyn Lloyd, when he said that 'in the domestic field there would be no feeling of security if the leading criminals were merely to announce their intention not to rob with violence.'[37] In every case the Western governments wanted inspection to precede or to proceed simultaneously with disarmament, whilst the Soviet Union wanted disarmament to precede verification.

Verification was a major cause of East-West disagreement from 1946 to 1963. The battle began on 14 June 1946 when Bernard Baruch submitted the United States' plan to the United Nations for the international ownership and control of all nuclear facilities to ensure that they were not being used for military purposes. The Soviet representative, Mr Gromyko, countered with the Kremlin's plan five days later. This proposed the negotiation of a convention stipulating,

> the prohibition of the production and employment of atomic weapons, the destruction of existing stocks of atomic weapons and the condemnation of all activities undertaken in violation of the convention.[38]

Subsequently, Mr Gromyko argued there should be 'other measures aiming at the establishment of methods to ensure the strict observance of the terms and obligations contained in the above mentioned convention . . . ' Deadlock ensued over the United States' insistence that international ownership of nuclear facilities was essential and

Soviet insistence that any investigatory body should come under the Security Council where it had a veto. The stalemate spread to conventional armaments after the Commission for Conventional Armaments was established by the UN on 13 February 1947.

All this was shadow boxing as it was difficult even to imagine a world in which some of the far-reaching measures of disarmament proposed had taken place or in which the Soviet Union was really open to hordes of international inspectors. The problems were only partly solved in the 1960s, when the construction of reconnaissance satellites and the acceptance of the desirability of limited disarmament measures, for the first time made progress possible. These changes brought about the Partial Test Ban Treaty in 1963, which could be verified by monitoring outside the Soviet Union, and the first Strategic Arms Limitation Treaty in 1972 which could be verified by satellites.

Sanctions

Even if breaches of an international agreement were detected this would by no means solve the problem. According to Lord Noel Baker,

> if Russia or a Russian ally were proved to have infringed the treaty, the most important sanction would lie in the fact that the other nations would forthwith cease to disarm . . . In any case collective economic and financial measures are the right preliminary answer to a violation of a disarmament treaty and they should be organised in advance.[39]

However, neither the fact that other states might cease to disarm, nor the threat of collective economic sanctions is likely to deter a state determined to break an agreement. Economic sanctions have been notoriously unsuccessful when they have been tried — against Italy in 1935, against Rhodesia in the 1960s and 1970s or against the Soviet Union after the invasion of Afghanistan in December 1979 and after the imposition of military rule in Poland in December 1981. In each case proponents of sanctions argued that they would have worked if all states had co-operated. But this is precisely what they cannot be relied upon to do. Indeed, the more effective they are, the more any country breaking the sanctions is likely to benefit from doing so.

Furthermore, as we shall see, the evidence of evasion of an arms control agreement is always likely to be vague and often extremely technical. Moreover, there will invariably be a section of public opinion in a democracy which argues that the evidence should be ignored because it will damage relations with the malefactor. Thus, in a democratic state it will take a long time before a decision can be taken to reverse a trend towards disarmament and to begin to rearm, in the face of a power determined to breach its international obligations. Although Adolf Hitler came to power in January 1933 and, although he made no secret before he seized power of his intention to overturn the Versailles settlement, yet it was not until three years later that Britain began to build up its armaments to any great extent.[40] The Soviet Union by contrast, being unconstrained by any but strictly strategic considerations, was able to respond immediately to Hitler's seizure of power.

Whilst democracies will very often deliberately overlook breaches of international agreements, if the international atmosphere darkens beyond a certain point, it is doubtful whether even intrusive inspection will convince deeply hostile states that arms control agreements are being observed. The sole international inspection system covering every continent is that administered by the International Atomic Energy Agency (IAEA) for the Nuclear Non Proliferation Treaty (NPT). Iraq is a party to this treaty and its nuclear facilities are inspected by officials of the IAEA. The inspection system is intrusive and amounts to precisely the sort of measure which the Russians rejected on the grounds that it was espionage. The Soviet Union does not therefore allow IAEA inspection even of its civil nuclear installations – unlike Britain and the United States.

Yet, on 8 June 1981 nine Israeli F16 and six F 15s destroyed the nuclear reactor which the French were building near Baghdad for the Iraqis. The Israelis argued that it was going to be used for producing nuclear weapons, even though it was subject to IAEA safeguards specifically designed to prevent this. Some would argue that the raid was purely to help Mr Begin's Israeli government win the impending elections and that it says little about the adequacy of IAEA inspection or about Iraq's nuclear ambitions. But this is not so. It is clear that international inspection failed to satisfy the Israelis. A total of 82.9 per cent of the Israelis interviewed in one opinion poll thought that the raid was justified.[41] Moreover, there were certain suspicious aspects of the projected Iraqi reactor. It was designed to operate on highly enriched fuel that could be diverted to weapons manufacture. The French government itself would have preferred to supply a reactor which only required uranium enriched to 20 per cent. But the Iraqis were reluctant to accept this. Finally, two weeks after the Israeli raid, the Iraqi

President called on all 'peace and security-loving nations of the world' to help the Arabs build an atomic bomb to counter Israel's purported nuclear arsenal.

What would happen to the Arabs and humanity if Israel were to impose conditions and the Arabs refused them and Israel would then use the Atomic bomb against the Arabs because of this?[42]

In these circumstances it was not surprising that there was a good deal of sympathy for the Israelis in other countries. The chairman of the Zionist Federation of Great Britain wrote to *The Times*, one

> cannot be so naive as to be deluded and expect your readers to be deluded by the mere fact of Iraq having signed the Non Proliferation Treaty. Fair-minded commentators and historians . . . will no doubt be thinking of the piece of paper which Mr Chamberlain with more optimism than reality brought back from Munich![43]

Similarly the novelist, Alan Sillitoe, wrote to the paper, 'international guarantees cannot ensure the safety of Israel. Only eternal vigilance on the part of Israel itself can attempt to do that'.[44] *The Times* argued that the Israeli attack showed the need to improve IAEA safeguards but, however much these were improved, the need for some degree of trust would remain. Disarmament agreements by themselves cannot be expected to dispel years of mistrust and suspicion.

Alva Myrdal, the Swedish writer on disarmament, has made the claim that,

> the overriding assumption must be that any government that has negotiated a disarmament (or nonarmament) agreement . . . will enter as a party to the agreement with no intention of breaking it or of cheating. The historical record speaks for the validity of this assumption. It is doubtful, in fact, that there has ever been an instance of a clandestine violation in the arms field . . . [45]

Evidently, and quite rightly, the Israelis felt differently. As we have seen, Mrs Myrdal's claim is certainly very far from true of the interwar period. She may, however, have been speaking of the period from 1945 to 1963 when few arms control agreements were in force. Even here, however, there was controversy. The Chinese, Russians and North Koreans accused US forces of using biological weapons in Korea in

1952 and 1953.[46] Admittedly the United States was not a party to the Geneva Protocol and therefore it could have used biological weapons without infringing international law. But the accusations were made because of the widespread feeling that the use of such weapons was barbarous and illegal. The Russians now appear to have retracted their accusations. However, they reflected the difficulty of proving or disproving such statements and the likelihood that accusations of that sort will be made when relations are bad enough – thus emphasising once again the link between arms control and politics. Finally, as we shall see in the next chapter, the controversy surrounding purported breaches of arms control agreements has gradually intensified.

Notes

1. For Eden's own views see *The Memoirs of Sir Anthony Eden, Full Circle*, Cassell, London, 1960. See also the obituary of Mr Selwyn Lloyd in *The Times*, 18 May 1978, and B. Levin, 'Lord Mountbatten and the Suez Fiasco', *The Times*, 5 November 1980.
2. James A. Nathan, 'A Fragile detente: the U2 incident re-examined', *Military Affairs*, October 1975.
3. 'Graver Turn in Cuba Crisis', *Guardian*, 27 October 1962.
4. 'The fears that Whiskey brought to the surface', *Guardian*, 7 November 1981; 'Spurning the easy way out', *Guardian*, 31 October 1981; 'N-weapons on Soviet submarine', *Guardian*, 6 November 1981.
5. FO/83/1704, memorandum by Sir John Ardagh, 7 June 1899.
6. R.D. Burns, 'Origins of the United States' Inspection policy', *Disarmament and Arms Control*, p. 159.
7. Ibid.
8. Major General A.C. Temperley, *The Whispering Gallery of Europe*, Collins, London, 1939, p. 66.
9. Burns, 'Origins', pp. 161-2.
10. *Documents on German Foreign Policy*, Series C, Volume 1, HMSO, 1957, no. 259, Ambassador in the US to Neurath, 23 May 1933.
11. AIR/5/1099, letter from E.H. Carr in Geneva to the Foreign Office, 23 November 1932.
12. AIR papers loc. cit., Disarmament Conference 1932, Ministerial Committee, Supervision, 16 December 1932.
13. AIR papers loc. cit., Admiralty memorandum.
14. WO/32/4091, Temperley minute of 17 November 1933.
15. See Note 12 supra.
16. WO/32/4091.
17. AIR/5/1114, note by Brigadier Temperley, 18 January 1934. See also WO/32/4091, minute of 23 November 1933.
18. WO/32/4091, minute of 20 September 1933.
19. AIR/5/1114, Disarmament Conference 1932, Ministerial Committee, Supervision, 23 May 1934, para. 22.
20. Loc. cit., para. 28.

21. Loc. cit., para. 41.

22. Treaty series, No 5, 1924, Cmd, 2036, p. 11.

23. G. Bennett, *Naval Battles of World War II*, Batsford, London, 1975, p. 18 passim.

24. G. Till in P. Towle (ed.), *Estimating Foreign Military Power*, Croom Helm, London, 1982, p. 180.

25. E.J. Gumbel in S. Melman (ed.), *Inspection for Disarmament*, Columbia University Press, 1958, p. 203 passim. See also P. Noel Baker, *The Arms Race*, Calder, London, 1958, p. 534 passim.

26. AIR/5/398, Supervision by the League of Nations of the Demilitarization of the Rhineland, 17 December 1926.

27. Gumbel, in *Inspection for Disarmament*. See also AIR/5/427.

28. AIR papers loc. cit., note of 12 January 1926.

29. WO/32/4097, report of November 1929.

30. G. Till in *Estimating Foreign Military Power*, p. 182.

31. AIR/5/427, letter from the President of the Conference of Ambassadors, 23 May 1934.

32. Loc. cit., Final Report of the Liquidation Board, 31 January 1928.

33. Burns, 'Origins', p. 166 passim.

34. 804 meeting of the UN First Committee, 6 December 1955.

35. Joan Beaumont, 'A Question of Diplomacy', *RUSI Journal*, September 1973.

36. 580 meeting of the UN First Committee, 20 March 1953.

37. 658 meeting of the UN First Committee, 6 November 1953.

38. *Documents on Disarmament*, Vol. 1, Department of State, Washington, 1960, p. 17.

39. P. Noel Baker, *The Arms Race*, Calder, London, 1958, p. 544.

40. H. Montgomery Hyde, *British Air Policy Between the Wars*, Heinemann, London, 1976, p. 318 passim.

41. 'Most Israelis backed Iraq raid', *The Times*, 27 June 1981.

42. 'Iraq seeks help to build atom bombs', *The Times*, 24 June 1981.

43. *The Times*, 18 June 1981.

44. Loc. cit., 12 June 1981.

45. Alva Myrdal, 'The International Control of Disarmament', *Scientific American*, October 1974.

46. *Documents on Disarmament*, Vol. 1, p. 372.

11 VERIFICATION – THE EXPERIENCE OF THE 1970s

In the 1960s and 1970s there was a widespread belief in the West that one of the main purposes of the arms control negotiations and treaties was to enhance confidence between East and West and thus to consolidate the process of detente. Many of the arms control agreements negotiated in that period, such as the Seabed Treaty which banned the emplacement of nuclear, chemical and biological weapons on the seabed, had only a limited effect on the weapons possessed by NATO and the Warsaw Pact. On the other hand, they gave the public reason to hope that East-West relations would gradually improve.

There have always been those who thought that arms control negotiations would have the opposite effect. Thus, Winston Churchill argued in the 1920s and 1930s that such discussions made nations more neurotic about their defences and focused attention on discrepancies between force levels:

> the elaborate process of measuring swords around the table at Geneva . . . stirs all the deepest suspicions and anxieties of the various powers, and forces all statesmen to consider all sorts of hypothetical contingencies which but for this prolonged process perhaps would not have crossed their minds and would only have remained buried in the archives of some general staff.[1]

It is certainly true to say that, whilst the SAL negotiations have been going on, there has been intense scrutiny amongst Western experts of the state of the US-Soviet military balance. SALT was taking place whilst the Russians· were drawing level (and some would say moving ahead) of the United States in strategic systems but the talks have not been the main cause of this change. Moreover, the public would have concentrated on this development whether or not arms control negotiations were in progress. Similarly in Europe the public has taken a spasmodic interest in the balance of forces in the theatre. But this interest predated the MBFR negotiations and was largely the result of the Western belief that the Russians were greatly superior in conventional forces.

The evidence, therefore, suggests that the public takes an interest in armaments when potential enemies appear to be increasing in power and when the international atmosphere is darkening, rather than when disarmament negotiatons are in progress. On the official level disarmament negotiations evidently improve relations between those actually involved. This is partly because they very often acquire a vested interest in the success of the discussions. Thus, the British representative at the first Hague Peace Conference reported,

> many of the delegates assembled at the Hague entered upon their duties with the conviction that nothing particular would come of their labours and that [it] would end in the expression of benevolent sentiments . . . but before they had been at work a fortnight a remarkable change came over the spirit of the conference.[2]

Similarly one of the members of the British delegation to the League conferences noted of Lord Cushendun, the British representative,

> he soon became susceptible to Geneva influences. When he first came out he remarked that what the Admiralty said was good enough for him . . . It was interesting to watch his metamorphosis. As time went and he heard the other side, he became a severe critic of the more extreme pretensions of some of the Service departments.[3]

Thus, delegates from different, and even potentially opposing, states acquire a vested interest in the success of the negotiations with which they are involved. They also begin to sympathise with other diplomats because of the common bonds of professionalism. Generally, though not universally, negotiations improve relations at the diplomatic level.

We can therefore dismiss the idea that the actual process of negotiating arms control agreements worsens international relations. But this leaves open the question whether arms control treaties can cause international frictions. As we have seen, the 1960s and 1970s saw the signature of a whole series of partial arms control agreements between East and West. Experience since that time suggests that arms control agreements enhance confidence when East-West relations are otherwise satisfactory but that, when relations start to deteriorate, they may contribute to this deterioration if they are inadequately verified. Evidence of ambiguities in the way that the Soviet Union has abided by its obligations under these treaties accumulates. When detente is in the ascendant these are ignored. As detente becomes more precarious, and particularly in the atmosphere prevailing after the Soviet invasion of Afghanistan, such suspicions occupy the centre of the stage and are interpreted in a much less favourable light.

In July 1976 the Russians breached the 1936 Montreux Convention by sending the aircraft carrier, *Kiev*, through the Straits of the Dardanelles. Carriers are defined in the Convention as 'surface vessels of war, whatever their displacement, designed or adapted primarily for the purpose of carrying and operating aircraft at sea'. However, the Russians claimed that the *Kiev* was an anti-submarine cruiser and the Turks, who were isolated at that time because of their dispute with Greece over Cyprus, allowed the ship to pass. Western governments made murmurs of disapproval but in the atmosphere prevailing only a year after the Final Act of the CSCE was signed, they were unwilling to make formal protests for fear of damaging detente. There was some reaction amongst informed observers and, in a leading article, *The Times* suggested that Western governments should at least have made a formal protest but this advice was ignored and Soviet actions were quickly forgotten.[4] However, it was not until August 1982 that the Russians dropped any pretence that the *Kiev* and its sister ship were not aircraft carriers. They now called them 'air capable ships' and to stress their relative insignificance added 'for these two aircraft carriers, the United States has twenty'.[5]

If the passage of the *Kiev* showed that Western governments were prepared to ignore Soviet breaches of international agreements when detente was in the ascendant, the effects of the decline of detente were obvious in the evolution of governmental reaction to allegations that the Russians were systematically breaching the Biological Weapons Convention. The Convention came into force in March 1975. In September of that year the *Boston Globe* reported that the United States had obtained photographic evidence which suggested that in

> recent months the Soviet Union has been constructing or expanding facilities which appear to be biological arms productions plants, having very high incinerator stacks and large cold storage bunkers that could be used for stock-piling weapons.[6]

These allegations were repeated in June 1976. According to the *Daily Telegraph* US intelligence had located six plants situated on a railway running east of Moscow which were 'either suspected of producing and storing biological warfare materials or said to be capable of conversion from present agricultural uses'.[7] Since many factories could be

converted from civilian to military uses, the reference to possible agricultural uses greatly weakened the force of the allegations. However,
it was not so much weaknesses of this sort but the prevailing atmosphere which determined that the report would be ignored.

The allegations about Soviet breaches of the Biological Weapons
Convention only achieved wide press coverage in January 1978. Reuter
reported from Brussels that US satellites had located factories in the
Soviet Union 'which intelligence analysts conclude are research and production centres' for biological weapons. According to the same reports,
satellite photographs revealed 'heavily guarded complexes with equipment necessary to grow biological agents in cultures and railway lines
containing specially designed tanker waggons'.[8] The same intelligence
sources apparently believed that the Russians were 'working on refining
and making more lethal microbes and viruses causing the plague,
anthrax, tuberculosis, smallpox, yellow fever and diphtheria'. Such allegations could hardly have been based on satellite evidence. Many of the
diseases mentioned would also have been useless as weapons. But the
reports perhaps reflected concern that the progress of genetic engineering might make it possible to perfect more effective biological
weapons – a prospect discussed at a forum held by the US National
Academy of Sciences in March 1977.[9]

A Soviet representative attended this forum and in the previous
August East European experts had warned at discussions on 'new
weapons of mass destruction' in Geneva that genetic engineering might
lead to the production of new and very effective weapons which were
not covered by the Biological Weapons Convention. On 9 August 1976
Academician Fokin from the Soviet Union had argued that,

> one of the characteristics of the new types of mass destruction
> weapons now being developed was their potentially high selectivity
> of action, for instance disrupting certain functions in the human
> organism, affecting persons of a specific ethnic group or negatively
> affecting agricultural production by bringing about changes in
> certain types of plants and animals.

As far as human beings were concerned, Fokin warned that 'selectivity
could apply to distinctions in blood type, skin pigmentation, types of
food and ethnic appurtenances'. Because they were the result of new
genetic techniques, such weapons 'might be utilised to bypass existing
agreements and treaties'.

Fokin's concern that developments in genetic engineering could be used to produce new weapons was supported by Professor Böhme from East Germany. Böhme also warned that synthetic viruses could 'cause epidemic diseases for which no therapy yet existed'. Moreover, Böhme 'held that possible genetic weapons could be based on new biological principles of action not covered by the Biological Weapons Convention and which represented scientific findings in molecular biology and molecular and cell genetics'. The denials by Fokin and Böhme that such new weapons would be covered by the existing Convention produced strong protests from Dutch and British experts and Böhme subsequently retracted his claims and argued that all that was needed was strict observance of the existing Convention.

It is not clear why the East European representatives raised the question of using genetic engineering techniques to produce new weapons of mass destruction at that stage. They may have wanted to test Western reactions to the suggestion that such weapons were not covered by the Biological Weapons Convention. But they remained very sensitive to any allegation that they were themselves breaching the agreement. Following the January 1978 Reuter story, the Russians vehemently denied the existence of the factories described in the press reports. Tass described the reports as 'crude and vicious fabrications' and suggested that they were inventions of the British Foreign Office's 'misinformation department'.[10] The communist *Morning Star* said that 'the story bears the marks of yet another move by the faceless ones of NATO to whip up cold-war hysteria to justify their demands for more arms and the production and use of the neutron bomb'.[11] Once again, however, there was no official reaction from the Western side and the allegations were allowed to fade into the past.

This situation changed dramatically two years later. In 1979 reports began to appear in the West about one or more major accidents at two of the factories mentioned in the 1975 *Boston Globe* report. The accidents were supposed to have taken place at Berdsk near Novosibirsk in Siberia and at Kashino near Sverdlovsk in the Ural mountains. However, it was not until March 1980, following the Soviet invasion of Afghanistan and coincident with the convening of a review conference to examine the working of the Biological Weapons Convention, that the United States asked the Soviet Union to comment on the press reports. A US spokesman explained the delay in questioning the Soviet Union by arguing that 'information about the Sverdlovsk incident had been compiled over a period by intelligence specialists and the United States only recently felt it had sufficient information to approach the Soviet Union about its concern.'[12] Nevertheless, there were some who denied that the timing of the allegations was coincidental. They argued that the reports were intended to halt the discussions with the Soviet Union on prohibiting the production of chemical weapons by reducing confidence in Soviet integrity.[13]

The Soviet Union described the allegations as 'impudent slanders' and Russian officials maintained that a natural outbreak of anthrax was to blame for the deaths in Sverdlovsk.[14] They also argued that attempts to cast doubt upon the Soviet Union's good faith could 'shatter current international accords and complicate the efforts of states to curb the arms race'. US officials described the Soviet response as serious but evidently continued to harbour grave doubts about its veracity. Nor was this entirely surprising in view of the contradictory nature of Soviet statements. The deputy chief doctor of the main Sverdlovsk hospital denied to Western reporters that there had been any outbreak of anthrax in the city.[15] An editor of the Sverdlovsk newspaper admitted that his journal had tried to educate the public about the disease by carrying three articles on ways of dealing with 'Siberian ulcers', the Soviet designation for one type of anthrax, but denied this was connected with an outbreak of the disease. The Soviet authorities themselves claimed that the outbreak was of the intestinal variety and was caused by the mishandling of food.[16] However, intestinal anthrax is usually found amongst primitive people since it is caught by eating uncooked meat. Moreover, the spring of 1979 was an unlikely time for an anthrax outbreak since they usually take place during a hot summer following a wet spring, whilst the winter of 1978-9 had been particularly cold.

How useful would anthrax be as a weapon? It can be fatal if it is not treated promptly. Moreover, it might be mistaken for influenza in its early stages[17] and, even if it were identified, it is not certain that pulmonary anthrax responds to standard medicines such as penicillin. An aggressor wishing to use anthrax could vaccinate his own troops against the disease and Soviet scientists are known to have been working for many years on vaccines against anthrax. A high proportion of recent articles about anthrax in medical journals have been written by East European and Soviet specialists, probably because the disease is still prevalent in their countries.[18] Improvement in vaccines could make it possible for Western armies also to prepare against anthrax but the West would first have to be convinced that the prospect of the Soviet Union making use of such weapons was a real one. In one sense the very longevity of anthrax spores in infected ground makes it a dubious weapon for a state to use which wishes to expand its empire.

British experts spread anthrax spores on Gruinard Island off the coast of Scotland during the Second World War to test their effectiveness and the island is still infected.[19] On the other hand, the same objection could be raised against nuclear weapons because of the long-lived radiation which they produce.

Neither the confusion in Soviet comments on events in Sverdlovsk, nor the reports published in Western newspapers, prove that the Russians are breaching the Biological Weapons Convention. Even if an accident occurred at a laboratory this would not prove Soviet guilt because parties are permitted to produce small quantities of agents to test protective measures. But the scale of the outbreak is crucial and some press reports have suggested that hundreds of deaths occurred: 'transmission of anthrax from one human being to another has never been recognised'.[20] Thus, such small quantities of spores from a laboratory accident could not cause an epidemic. On the other hand, it is perfectly possible for spontaneous outbreaks to occur. Infected anthrax spores retain their virulence in the ground for many years and anthrax has often occurred naturally in Siberia – as it has in many other parts of the world including Australia and the United States.[21] Sverdlovsk was not, however, the most likely place for such an outbreak since they usually take place in the damp, low-lying areas near rivers and the city is several hundred feet above sea level. Thus, because of the location, the timing and the alleged nature of the illness, the Soviet explanation appears unlikely. But this does not prove that the Russians were breaking the BW Convention, it only suggests that they did not want to say precisely what had actually taken place.

Whilst the Western media were reporting the purported epidemic near Sverdlovsk, they were also reporting allegations that Soviet troops and Soviet allies in Afghanistan and South East Asia had used gases against insurgents. In November 1979 there were press reports that a 'US defence Department medical team had found that poison gas had been used against the hill tribes in Laos that have resisted communist control'.[22] The team's preliminary report suggested that nerve gas, as well as a gas causing massive bleeding, and a less powerful riot control agent had been used. In March 1980 a surgeon with a Red Cross team on the Thai-Kampuchean border also came to the conclusion that the Vietnamese were using chemical weapons. 'I did not believe the Vietnamese were using poison gas before conducting the atopsy [on the bodies of six Kampuchean rebels] but I now believe that such gas has been used', he was reported as saying. His allegations were supported by those who carried out post mortems at refugee camps on the frontier in September and October 1981.[23] Apart from such medical reports, much of the evidence for the use of chemical agents is derived from allegations by refugees, many of whom claim to have been atttacked long before they made their reports. Nevertheless, one journalist claimed in 1981:

> few who have interviewed Hmong refugees have any doubt that, if the details of the individual accounts appear muddled, the substance of what they are reporting is accurate; that they have been the target of persistant air attacks involving the use of biological or chemical agents.[24]

In particular there are allegations that mycotoxins have been employed. These are poisons which can be produced naturally but which can also be manufactured in large quantities. Mycotoxins can cause vomiting within seconds of infection, multiple bleeding of the mucus membranes, bloody diarrhoea, severe itching and tingling of the skin. Death can occur within minutes and the locations affected will remain dangerous for some time.

Despite the number of allegations, a UN investigatory team under Major General Esmat Ezz of Egypt was unable either to disprove or prove the various claims. Blood and urine samples taken from those who claimed to have been attacked showed no abnormalities that would normally follow exposure to poisonous chemicals. The team found language problems in communicating with the refugees on the Thai frontier and it was particularly sceptical of allegations that chemical weapons were being rained down from a great height since it felt that agents would have been dispersed long before they hit the ground. Some scientists have also shown a good deal of scepticism about the refugees' reports and the idea that mycotoxins could be taken back to US laboratories for examination. One said that samples had been 'collected under unspecified conditions and transported without proper precautions against contamination . . . No scientist independent of the government would consider such a specimen to constitute scientific evidence . . . ' The United States withdrew allegations that mycotoxins do not occur naturally in hot countries such as Vietnam and Kampuchea and a research team from the university of Maryland showed that they were very prevalent in parts of Brazil.[25]

Similar problems dogged attempts to substantiate claims that 3,000 people had been killed in Afghanistan in 47 separate chemical weapon attacks between the summer of 1979 and the summer of 1981. The UN team investigating the allegations visited Afghan refugee camps at Peshawar and Quetta in February 1982. The reports which they heard there from refugees were very similar to those which they had heard in South East Asia. One refugee told the team:

> in June 1981 . . . there was a gas attack. The Russians brought a tank to the hole, lowered a pipe into the hole and poured gas. Ten people who were close to the gas died and their bodies were swollen and they had nose bleeds. Others had diarrhoea, dizziness and nausea . . . Those who were close died within five minutes.[26]

Reports of the use of chemical and biological weapons have to be treated with great caution precisely because they are frequently greeted with outrage and horror. Moreover, many high explosives release chemicals which can asphyxiate those in the area. And it is difficult for anyone without medical training, let alone unsophisticated villagers, to be certain about the causes of deaths in combat. An article in the *New Statesman* described the allegations about Soviet activities in Afghanistan as 'black propaganda' which was designed to damage the Soviet image and to persuade the US Congress to vote funds for the production of binary chemical weapons.[27] The article suggested that all the allegations about Soviet activities in Afghanistan were based on a secondhand report by one defecting Afghan army officer. It also quoted a British television camerman, who had spent four months in Afghanistan and who had considerable military experience, as saying that the allegations were based on misunderstandings about the effects of high explosive.

In 1928 the Soviet Union adhered to the Geneva Protocol which bans the use of chemical and biological weapons in warfare. However, neither Laos nor Afghanistan are parties to the Convention and it is only binding in international wars between parties. Thus, in some cases, what is at stake may not be a formal breach of the Geneva Protocol as such. On the other hand, dislike of the use of chemical weapons is strong and widespread, and Vietnam and the Soviet Union have both protested angrily against allegations that they are making use of such weapons. Soviet credibility over Afghanistan has, however, been reduced by its poor public relations campaign. Few outside the Soviet Union will believe the claim made by the Soviet news agency, Tass, on 3 January 1980 that the late President Amin of Afghanistan was 'in the service of the CIA'. Similarly, claims by Soviet embassies around the world that Afghan insurgents have been using grenades containing lethal agents and marked 'made in the USA' appear equally improbable.[28] The important aspect of the allegations about Soviet and Vietnamese use of chemical and biological weapons is that they have been supported by Western governments and particularly by the USA. This would have been unthinkable at the height of detente. In June 1980 the USA supplied a 125-page document to the UN containing all the available allegations about the use of CBW. In September 1981 Mr Haig, the US Secretary of State, said during a visit to Berlin that the USA was very concerned about reports of lethal gases being used in South East Asia and Afghanistan. He claimed that US officials had located abnormally high levels of lethal mycotoxins in South East Asia and that they suspected that these were the 'yellow rain' described by refugees as falling during Vietnamese attacks.[29] Not surprisingly the Soviets and Vietnamese utterly repudiated Mr Haig's allegations. A few years previously this sort of wrangle would have been inconceivable. Allegations about the use of chemical and biological weapons would have been ignored by governments. Even if they believed that they had substance, they would have been too troubled by the fear of damaging detente to raise them officially. By 1980 such fears no longer had any effect.[30]

While there was still some hope of reviving detente, Western governments also played down the significance of allegations that the Russians had breached SALT 1. These allegations increased in intensity and frequency until in November 1977 former US Defense Secretary, Melvin Laird, added his voice to the protests. Laird claimed,

among some in the Ford Administration evidently, the desire to see detente work was so intense that they sought to suppress, or at least minimize, the significance of the intelligence revealing Soviet violations.[31]

Divisions within the US government about the extent and significance of any Soviet violations of the SALT 1 agreements were reflected in an official background briefing provided in February 1978. The briefing claimed that 'the US does not feel that the Soviet Union has violated either the letter or the spirit of the Treaty since it was signed on May 26, 1972'.[32] However, it went on to admit that the US had made eight specific inquiries about Soviet activities under the treaty and the general tone of the briefing suggested that the Russians had pushed the treaty as far as they dared to go and had only desisted from certain activities because of US protests. For example, concealment of activities related to strategic weapons was prohibited under the treaty. In 1974 the United States came to the conclusion that the Russians were increasingly trying to conceal some of their activities and US officials protested accordingly. As a result 'early 1975 careful analysis of intelligence information on activities in the USSR led the US to conclude that there no longer appeared to be an *expanding* pattern of concealment' (my italics).

The ABM Treaty, which was signed at the same time as SALT 1, laid down that no missiles, launchers or radars were to be tested in 'an ABM mode' other than those specifically permitted under the agreement. In 1973 and 1974 US officials came to believe that the radar associated with SA-5 surface-to-air missiles was being used in this way. The Russians denied this but shortly afterwards ceased the disputed activity. The US also believed that the Russians had maintained a greater number of ABM launchers than was permitted under the treaty and that they had also not dismantled old ICBM launchers and SLBMs fast enough to comply with SALT. The Russians admitted that this was so but subsequently complied with the agreement. There are various possible explanations for such infringements. Either they were relatively unimportant breaches caused by Soviet bureaucratic inertia or incompetence, or they were deliberately carried out on the assumption that they would not be detected or to test the efficacy of US intelligence methods.

Were detente still a popular rallying cry, the ambiguities in Soviet behaviour under international agreements would arouse very little interest. One could argue that the infringement of the Montreux Convention was relatively unimportant and that the alleged breaches in the Biological Weapons Convention remain unproven. Similarly one could argue that there is no firm evidence that lethal chemicals have been used in Laos, Kampuchea and Afghanistan and that, even if such evidence were available, the USSR would not have breached the Geneva Protocol. Moreover, the Russians have responded appropriately to US complaints about SALT 1 and they have also carried out their obligations under the terms of the CSCE, albeit grudgingly.[33]

Furthermore, critics of the West could argue that there have been some ambiguities in Western behaviour. The original allegations that the Soviet Union was building biological weapons factories were made in the same month that the CIA was discovered to have 'secretly maintained a stockpile of deadly shell fish toxin and [to have] ignored a Presidential decree that all toxins be destroyed'.[34] The Russians also made various inquiries about US observance of SALT 1. In particular they asked whether the missile silos for old Atlas and Titan missiles could be reactivated.[35] They protested against covering placed over US missile silos so that they could be hardened during bad weather and they questioned the purpose of a new US radar in Alaska which they suspected could be used to help US ABM defences.

While the United States was questioning the Soviet Union about its alleged use of chemical weapons in Afghanistan, press reports suggested that the United States had itself planned to use chemical weapons during the abortive attempt to free the US diplomats held captive in Teheran. Critics could argue that this was a more obvious plan to breach the Geneva Protocol than Soviet activities in Afghanistan because Iran, unlike Afghanistan, is a party to the Geneva Protocol. The press reports have also been ambiguous about the weapons which the US rescue team planned to use. Some press reports suggested that these contained 'nondeadly paralysing gas', others that they contained 'incapacitating gas', and yet others that they held a 'debilitating gas'.[36] The distinctions are important because the United States has renounced the use of incapacitating chemical weapons in warfare but specifically retains the right to use less powerful irritating agents. Apart from such ambiguities, supporters of the United States could argue that it was not actually at war with Iran and therefore that the Geneva Protocol did not apply (although Russophiles could argue that this is also true of operations in Afghanistan). The agents involved were to have been used against the hostages' unofficial captors within the US embassy, and the Iranian Government could hardly claim that the captors were under its command without abandoning the pretence that they were not responsible for their actions.

Nevertheless, while there have been some ambiguities in Western behaviour under the arms control agreements currently in force, these ambiguities appear more limited than their Soviet equivalents. If the CIA did retain lethal biological agents after the Biological Weapons Convention came into force, then these were rapidly discovered, publicised by Western media and destroyed within the time allowed by the Convention. If the Soviet Union had doubts about Western behaviour under SALT 1, these doubts appear to have been quickly resolved. On the other hand, doubts about the way the Soviet Union had abided by its obligations are a natural result of its closed totalitarian society, its willingness to tell blatant lies over the political affiliations of the former President of Afghanistan and its refusal to accept international inspection of its territories or to explain its actions.

It would, in theory, be very easy for the Soviet Union to pull the rug out from under the feet of those who accuse it of breaching the Biological Weapons Convention if it were innocent of such breaches. The Soviet government can hardly be aware which of its factories give rise to Western concerns and it could explain their purpose and open them to inspection. The location of the factories and their external appearance have been described. Moreover, the Russians should also be aware that, while in a period of detente the scale of the alleged Soviet breaches – amounting to six major factories – made the reports less credible, as detente fades, the scale of these operations only appears the more frightening. But the Russian passion for secrecy is such that their failure to reveal the true nature of the factories cannot be taken as clear evidence of guilt. The situation as regards breaches in the Biological Weapons Convention was perhaps best summed up by *The Times*,

> perhaps Soviet indignation is justified but in the absence of any hard evidence either way suspicions are bound to linger, which could in time invalidate the spirit of trust and international confidence that the Convention was supposed to foster.[37]

Those who placed faith in the confidence building aspects of arms control negotiations hoped that their effects would be cumulative. Negotiations would take place enhancing confidence between East and West. Such confidence would enable limited arms control agreements to be negotiated. These would in turn enhance international confidence and make possible more far-reaching measures of disarmament. Experience has shown that the process is actually much more complex. The arms control negotiations did lead to limited agreements in the 1960s and 1970s. However, before the negotiators could attempt anything more ambitious, relations between NATO and the Warsaw Pact began to deteriorate. In these circumstances those groups which had been warning that the Russians were not abiding by their agreements began to be heard. The worse East-West relations became, the more credence was given to allegations that the Soviet Union was in breach of its commitments.

Today it is the turn of those who advocate detente, because of their trust in the Soviet Union or their fear that confrontation could lead to war, to feel that their opinions are ignored. It is not so much that harder evidence has accumulated about Soviet breaches of its international agreements as that the receptivity to such evidence has increased. Conversely, receptivity to arguments for detente has been reduced. The one incontrovertible breach of an agreement by the

Soviet Union occurred in 1976 with the passage of the *Kiev* through the Dardanelles. Most of the subsequent allegations about Soviet behaviour could only be finally decided one way or another by inspection of Soviet territory or examination of casualties in Afghanistan and South East Asia, which the Soviet Union is most unlikely to accept. Yet, short of such inspection, arms control may continue to contribute to the decline of international confidence just as it once contributed to its enhancement.

The relationship between arms control agreements and the general political situation can be compared to the relationship between the flywheel attached to the motor and the car itself. The flywheel is set in motion by the engine but once it has begun to move it prolongs the car's motion in any direction. Similarly, arms control agreements may have exacerbated or enhanced existing tendencies towards detente when detente was popular, and to the extent that they are inadequately verified away from detente today.

Notes

1. W. Churchill, *Arms and the Covenant*, Harrap, London, 1938, p. 64.
2. FO/83/1703, report of 31 July 1899.
3. Major General A.C. Temperley, *The Whispering Gallery of Europe*, Collins, London, 1939, p. 80.
4. E. Young, 'Soviet naval movements', letter in *The Times*, 27 July 1976. See also 'The Kiev breaks the Montreux Convention', editorial in *The Times*, 11 August 1976. See also P. Towle, 'The Montreux Convention as a regional arms control treaty – negotiation and practice', *Military Affairs*, October 1981.
5. *The Soviet Union: Facts, Problems, Appraisals*, Novosti, Moscow, 1982, pp. 113 and 132.
6. 'Russians suspected of germ-war violation', *Daily Telegraph*, 30 September 1975.
7. '6 Soviet works under germ war suspicion', *Daily Telegraph*, 16 June 1976.
8. 'Germ plant "seen by satellite" ', *Guardian*, 31 January 1978. 'New war germs "bred in Russia" ', *The Times*, 31 January 1978.
9. 'Fear as a new science steps into unknown', *Observer*, 13 March 1977.
10. 'Tass ridicules "germ weapon" reports', *Daily Telegraph*, 1 February 1978.
11. 'NATO tries germ war scare', *Morning Star*, 31 January 1978.
12. 'Soviet city "exposed to war germs" ', *Canberra Times*, 20 March 1980.
13. 'Anthrax and arms control', editorial in *International Herald Tribune*, 30 April 1980.
14. 'Germs', *Canberra Times*, 21 March 1980 and 'Anthrax outbreak natural', *Canberra Times*, 22 March 1980.
15. Ibid.
16. 'Killer germ "spread by food handling" ' *The Age*, 22 March 1980.
17. SIPRI, *The Problem of Chemical and Biological Warfare*, Volume 11,

Humanities Press, New York, 1973, p. 65 passim.
    18. See, for example, B.L. Cherkassi, 'Modern problems in the prevention of anthrax', *Journal of Microbiology, Epidemology and Immuno-biology*, August 1979. See also loc. cit., April 1979, S.B. Simonovich *et al.*, 'confinement of anthrax foci to soil-landscape zones in Rostov Province'. See also loc. cit., September 1978, G.M. Mashilova *et al.*, 'standardisation of the seeding material in producing live anthrax vaccine'.
    19. Robin Clarke, *The Silent Weapons*, David McKay, New York, 1968, p. 76.
    20. T.R. Harriman *et al.* (eds.), *Principles of Liberal Medicine*, McGraw Hill, New York, 1966, pp. 1583-4.
    21. Ibid.
    22. 'Poison gas "used against Lao tribes" ', *Canberra Times*, 26 November 1979.
    23. 'Viets "using poison gas in Kampuchea" ', *Australian*, 24 March 1980. See also 'Hanoi's use of poison "confirmed" ', *The Times*, 27 October 1981, and 'Vietnam denies US chemical war charge', *Guardian*, 17 September 1981.
    24. 'Refugees bring evidence of chemical warfare', *Guardian*, 16 September 1981. See also letter dated 11 April 1980 from the Permanent Representative of Democratic Kampuchea to the UN, A/35/173,S/13891, 15 April 1980.
    25. 'Yellow rain finding dubious', *The Times*, 25 November 1981; 'Hanoi's use of poison "confirmed"',*The Times*, 27 October 1981; 'Vietnam denies US chemical war charge', *Guardian*, 17 September 1981; 'Scientists wary of "yellow rain claims" ', *The Times*, 20 November 1981; 'Russia is "using chemical weapons" ', *Guardian*, 15 September 1981; 'Nerve gas report', *Canberra Times*, 14 January 1980.
    26. 'Chemical-Biological Warfare in Afghanistan', *Wall Street Journal*, 7 June 1982.
    27. Gwynne Roberts, 'The Campaign of misinformation', *New Statesman*, 4 April 1980.
    28. The *Tass* report of 3 January 1980 is reprinted in *Survival*, March/April 1980, p. 69. For allegations about Afghan use of US weapons, see 'Olympics set for technical chaos', *Canberra Times*, 19 April 1980, and 'Use of gas in Afghanistan', loc. cit., 8 May 1980.
    29. 'Haig claims evidence of chemical warfare in South-East Asia', *The Times*, 14 September 1981. 'Evidence by US of poison war', *The Times*, 15 September 1981.
    30. See also 'The yellow rain controversy', *The Times*, 16 September 1981; 'The coward's weapon, poison', *The Times*, 17 September 1981.
    31. 'SALT violations confirmed', *Aviation Week and Space Technology*, 12 December 1977. See also 'Arms pact violated repeatedly by Russia, US told', *Daily Telegraph*, 21 November 1977.
    32. Hugh Muir, 'Keeping a check on compliance with SALT I', United States Information Service, 2 March 1978.
    33. 'Implementation of the Helsinki accord June-November 1979', US Department of State Bureau of Public Affairs.
    34. See Note 6 supra.
    35. See Note 32 supra.
    36. 'Helicopter failure caused rescue mission to be aborted', *Canberra Times*, 27 April 1980; 'The Rescue that failed', *Sydney Morning Herald*, 28 April 1980.
    37. 'A matter of verification', editorial in *The Times*, 22 March 1980.

CONCLUSION

Political

If the last chapters have demonstrated anything it is that political and military detente must in the long run progress together or arms control will not progress at all. Not only is this true in the general sense but, as we shall see, the most successful negotiations incorporate both elements. In most cases agreements can only be negotiated between potential antagonists if political tensions are reduced. The non-aligned countries frequently assert that it is the Super Powers which are blocking the road to GCD. But, even if Super Power opposition could be overcome, this would only be one of the hurdles on the road to disarmament. The Arabs and Israelis, the Black and White African states, the Indians and Pakistanis, and the feuding groups in South East Asia will not reduce their armaments until their political antagonisms have subsided. Indeed, whilst the United States and the Soviet Union have been prepared to sit down and to discuss arms control throughout the Cold War, few of the antagonists listed above have been prepared to do so. When an Arab leader, such as President Sadat of Egypt, began negotiations with the Israelis, he was ostracised by his fellow Arabs and eventually assassinated.

Thus, most of the smaller feuding states have rejected any measures which could increase confidence between them. At the first UN Special Session on Disarmament in 1978 the Indian representative denied that his government would accept any CBMs to improve relations with Pakistan. At the Commonwealth Conference in Melbourne in October 1981, the Zimbabwe Prime Minister launched a bitter attack on President Reagan for improving US relations with South Africa. The state of mind of one of the feuding powers was best illustrated by the Saudi spokesman who told the UN,

> there was no need for the United Nations to concern itself with a disarmament plan for the Middle East, since the Middle East would scrap its armaments the moment the causes of the present trouble were removed, that is when Israel had departed from the area.[1]

The Saudi spokesman was tacitly ignoring many of the other causes of

163

war in the Middle East, apart from the Arab-Israeli conflict. But he was right to suggest that the solution of a political feud may lead to reduced armaments. A statesman who produces such a solution will, therefore, achieve more disarmament than one who sits in Geneva, Vienna or Helsinki discussing reductions in weaponry. If political passions cool and deep rifts are healed, and not replaced by new tensions, then armaments should gradually subside. This ought to be a truism but it is only too often ignored by the disarmament lobby. Conversely, the 'realists' very often implicitly assume that every current political dispute may continue indefinitely. Franco-German, or indeed Franco-British, relations should teach us that this is not so, even if we did not have the example of the dramatic improvement in US-Chinese relations from 1972 to 1982 to prove the contrary.

The Rush-Bagot Agreement

The task of the arms control and disarmament negotiations is very often to speed up or solidify improvements in political relations. To take the classic example, the war between Britain and America in 1812 showed that Britain had to reckon with United States' power. Conversely, it showed many Americans that they could not easily acquire Canada by force as they had expected to do.[2] Subsequently, most appreciated that boundary problems between the two countries would be better solved by diplomacy than by war. The conclusion of the 1812 war was, therefore, followed by a general political settlement and by the Rush-Bagot Agreement largely demilitarising the frontier and the Great Lakes in 1817. This disarmament agreement solidified US-British relations because it reduced fears that one side or the other would try to overturn the general political settlement by force.

There were only too many issues over which Britain and the USA could still quarrel when the war between them ended. For example, British soldiers and sailors captured by the US forces during the war had been deliberately released and dispersed in the hope that many would become settlers, to the chagrin of the British.[3] Worse still, some of the Black people serving in the British forces had been captured and sold into slavery.[4] After the end of the war British seamen continued to desert in the USA, whilst the British authorities in Quebec complained that the Americans were building fortifications in the area against agreement and to the anger of the Indians.[5] Similarly British merchants protested about US tariffs against their goods.[6] The multiple causes of friction can be contrasted with the desire amongst statesmen on both sides to improve relations. The British Foreign Minister, Lord

Castlereagh, wrote to Charles Bagot, the Minister in Washington in February 1817,

> you may say that it is the earnest wish of the government that its publick servants in the United States should be convinced that their first duty is to do all in their power for promoting the good understanding and harmony now happily subsisting between the two countries.[7]

When there were arguments with the Americans over Newfoundland fisheries, Castlereagh expressed his 'desire to come to an amicable understanding with the American government'[8] and when General Jackson executed British subjects in Florida, Castlereagh urged Bagot to continue his cautious and judicial handling of the issue.[9] On his side, Bagot made certain that, when the US President approached British territory in September 1817, 'every testimony of respect which the circumstances of the case would admit was shown to him by His Majesty's Officers at Fort George'.[10]

The innumerable opportunities for friction combined with the will amongst statesmen on both sides to minimise these, provided both the motive and the opportunity for an arms control agreement. The trigger for the US proposal appears to have been the insistence by Royal Naval ships on the Great Lakes on stopping US ships to see whether they were carrying illicit goods. James Monroe claimed that 'he received constant complaints of the conduct of British officers upon those waters in searching and interrupting the vessels of the United States'. Simultaneously the press, influenced by the US administration, campaigned bitterly against British activities 'in language at least very unfavourable to a temperate discussion . . . upon the subject'.[11] The United States made proposals both in London and in Washington to reduce tension on the Lakes. President Monroe argued that 'if each Nation should maintain on the lakes a large Naval Force, it would expose both to considerable and useless expense whilst it would multiply the risks of collision between them'.[12]

Castlereagh's immediate response to the US proposals was that any agreement should be of a general nature but Monroe argued for 'positive stipulations'. Bagot was surprised how far-reaching US ideas were when they were put on paper, so much that he began to suspect their intentions;

> I found them to include a proposal for a much larger reduction of

the Naval Force than seemed compatible with the ordinary business of a peace establishment, it contained certain restrictions on the employment of the vessels to be retained, which appeared to have some object in view beyond the one professed by the American government.[13]

Nevertheless, Bagot passed US ideas to London and there was thus a long hiatus from August 1816 to February 1817 whilst these were digested. Then Bagot was asked by Castlereagh to tell the US administration that Britain accepted its ideas, although the British pointed out that US proximity to the Lakes would give them an advantage in any construction after the agreement ended.[14] However, agreement was reached that most of the ships in service on the Lakes and the fortifications in the area should be dismantled 'forthwith'. The admirals were dilatory, perhaps because of their inherent suspicion of such agreements, in informing their commander on the spot, Robert Hall, that he should carry out the agreement. Accordingly he wrote to Bagot,

Your Excellency's authority is sufficient to command my immediate compliance with this arrangement and I have consequently sent orders to the different lakes, to call in and dismantle all but one schooner.[15]

The Rush-Bagot agreement by no means solved all United States-British problems in North America. A British report printed in the 1840s talked of the 'frequent collisions between British subjects and American citizens having taken place on the Disputed Territory between New Brunswick and the State of Maine'.[16] But Castlereagh, Monroe, Adams, Bagot and others had taken advantage of a unique moment at the end of a war when there was a profound willingness to put US-British relations on what they hoped was a permanently stable footing. The disarmament agreement was possible because there was political will to achieve it at the top, because there was enough friction to make such an agreement worthwhile, whilst there was not enough antagonism to make it impossible.

Chile-Argentine Agreement

A less well known agreement was negotiated by Chile and Argentina in 1902-3. The two countries had longstanding border disputes, although these had, for a time, appeared settled by a treaty negotiated in 1881. This laid down that the boundary should be the crest of the mountains

Conclusion   167

separating the two countries and this was also assumed to be the watershed:

> the boundary line shall run . . . over the highest summits of the said Cordilleras which divide the waters and shall pass between the sources flowing down to either side.[17]

When the watershed proved not to be on the summit, Argentina demanded that the boundary should run along the crests, whilst the Chilean government insisted that it should be along the watershed. Relations between the two countries steadily deteriorated. In May 1896 another agreement was reached 'after long and anxious negotiations in Santiago', but British ministers reported that it was received without satisfaction in Buenos Aires because 'it solves none of the points which have aroused angry feelings'.[18]

Chile appeared to be willing to submit the dispute to British arbitration but the Argentine government was more recalcitrant. However, steady pressure from Britain proved effective and in 1898 Queen Victoria was asked to arbitrate. An arbitration board was established with Lord Macnaghten, a Lord of Appeal, as President with Sir Thomas Holdich and Major General Sir John Ardagh as members.[19] When it began to meet it rapidly discovered that neither country had prepared its case and it was not until June 1900 that Buenos Aires produced the first two of its fat volumes of printed evidence.[20] In the meantime relations between the two countries remained tense. In February 1899 the British Minister in Santiago reported that the Chilean government would be happy to abandon the policy of 'armed peace which has established such a numerous expenditure in both countries'.[21] Yet in October 1901 the Argentines complained that the Chileans were building roads in the disputed area. The authorities in Santiago retorted that these were necessary for map-making in the region but the following month Buenos Aires broke off diplomatic relations.[22] Financial pressure was brought to bear on the antagonists by London, and the British government complained that any hostilities would be an insult to the arbitration tribunal. Under these pressures a tense peace was preserved.

Holdich left Britain for Latin America in January 1902 to survey the disputed areas — not always an easy task. Four months later he reported, 'we have been climbing slippery mountains and wading through bottomless . . . mud for a fortnight and we have seen some of the most magnificent scenery in the world.'[23] When he returned an award was made which was accepted by both parties. The steady improvement in relations as the tribunal's work proceeded allowed arms control negotiations to succeed in May 1902 and January 1903.[24] Ships under construction were to be sold. Those that could not be sold were to be completed and then placed under British care and no new ships were to be ordered for five years. Furthermore, in 'order to establish the just balance of the actual navies, Chile will disarm the "Capitain Prat" and the Argentine will disarm her two battleships, the "Garibaldi" and the "Pusyrredon" '. The three ships were to be tied up with all coal and ammunition removed and only caretaker crews left aboard. In consequence the Chilean naval budget in March 1903 showed a reduction of nearly 600,000 dollars in current expenditure and over 600,000 in future estimates.[25]

Frontier and disarmament agreements were followed by exchanges of military visits. In May 1903 the senior Chilean admiral and the Commander in Chief of the Army left Valparaiso for Buenos Aires. The same month Santiago celebrated the founding of the Argentine with speeches and torchlight processions: 'no effort was wanting on the part of the government and the upper classes to manifest the good relations now existing between the two countries'.[26] Inevitably difficulties continued; in 1903 there were riots in Chile and the USA threatened to send warships to protect its citizens. This provoked the Chileans to talk of retaining all their warships and there were even discussions and press stories about a grandiose Chile-Argentine-Brazil alliance to combat Washington.[27] Yet only two years later the Argentine Minister of Marine was worrying about Brazilian naval construction and ordering new small boats to protect Buenos Aires.[28]

Nevertheless, the Chile-Argentine naval agreement demonstrated what could be achieved. Without a boundary settlement there was no chance whatsoever of a disarmament agreement. But, if the political settlement had not been accompanied by an arms control treaty, not only would funds have been wasted but suspicions might have lingered. The reduction of naval forces was a very substantial token of goodwill.

Organisations

So far I have examined the main problems that arms control has to overcome, which are political. However, the methods employed to reach an agreement cannot be ignored. Because there were prolonged negotiations on arms control and disarmament in the interwar period and because discussions between East and West on these subjects have continued almost without intermission since 1945, we have a good deal of data on which to base conclusions. It is clear from this history that the structure of certain negotiations virtually precludes agreement on measures which would substantially reduce the military capabilities of the states involved, even if the political situation were reasonably favourable.

It has become the fashion over the last 20 years to isolate individual arms control issues which are deemed by some to be ripe for resolution and to carry on negotiations on these isolated issues. This fashion was a reaction to the situation in the late 1950s and early 1960s when negotiations centred round GCD. These far-reaching negotiations produced no agreement whatsoever, indeed they probably increased East-West tensions and suspicions because each side attacked the other for rejecting its proposals and attributed such rejections to the worst of motives. On the other hand, in the 1960s statesmen stumbled on a rich vein of peripheral issues on which agreement could be reached between East and West. As we have seen these were discussed at the Eighteen Nation Disarmament Conference (ENDC) and its successor the CCD in Geneva. The result was a series of treaties stretching from the Partial Test Ban signed in 1963 to the Environmental Modification Convention in 1977. None of these treaties greatly affected the military power of the Soviet Union or of the West, nor did they involve inspection on Soviet territory. But by the 1970s these peripheral agreements were starting to become harder to find. The CCD began again to discuss treaties which really might affect the Great Powers' military capability. This was the case with the Comprehensive Test Ban Treaty (CTBT) and with a ban on the production of CW.

The isolation of such issues appeals to two sets of individuals, the moralists and the civil servants. The moralists approve of the isolation of particular issues because they believe that there is an *a priori* case for banning napalm, for example, or for prohibiting nuclear tests in all environments.[29] All that is needed is goodwill, effort and perhaps public pressure and the approach is thus rationalist as well as moralistic. Civil servants support the isolation of particular issues because this makes them appear more manageable. A desk officer or department can be made responsible for a specific issue, such as the prohibition of chemical weapons, neat and tidy conferences can be arranged on the question with all the participants staying in the best hotels in Geneva, and the problem can be inscribed on the agenda of the CCD and the First Committee of the UN. The longer the discussions are prolonged, the more technical the issue will appear to be and therefore the more necessary for civil servants and serving officers to handle the issue rather than politicians.

Once this method of proceeding has been established, the moralists subsequently express astonishment that so little progress is made and blame this on the malevolence of governments, the military-industrial complex, communist Messianism, or whatever. A Yugoslav writer, Dusan Pirec, for example, attributes world tension and the failure of the arms control negotiations to the efforts by states to externalise internal conflicts:

> the increase of tension in international relations is resorted to as a buffer so that, through the increase of international tension, internal tension is decreased.[30]

Other commentators, such as the Romanian Sergiu Verona, attribute the absence of progress at the CCD to the 'lack of political will such a body should have'.[31] Consequently, those who hope for more far-reaching disarmament measures often collect petitions with innumerable signatures to impress their government and to stir it into action. Meanwhile the civil servants shake their heads and prepare for another round of working papers at the CCD on the verification of a ban on chemical weapons or on the prohibition of new weapons of mass destruction. Of course, sometimes progress is made by these methods but only on issues which do not affect the military power of those involved. Yet, some believe that by this process confidence will gradually be built up and that more far-reaching measures can then be attempted. The British Prime Minister, James Callaghan, told the first UN Special Session on Disarmament in June 1978

> Britain's approach is step by step, namely to persevere in placing the building blocks of peace one upon the other . . . the building blocks should be put in place so that they fit together, strengthen each other and produce a new base for further co-ordinated advance.[32]

The problem is that the ediface laboriously and slowly constructed may be broken down only too easily by tensions caused by such events as the invasion of Afghanistan.

It is, however, neither the malevolence of governments, nor any of the other conspiracies, which is responsible for the slow pace of the arms control negotiations but political hostilities, the intractable nature of the issues and the indequacy of the methods used to resolve them.

The fact is that hostile states reach agreement on major issues only by bargaining away areas where they are stronger than their potential enemies, in return for reductions in the areas where their potential enemies are more powerful. There is no easy way in which a bargain can be negotiated on one isolated matter. Either the Americans or the Russians will be ahead in terms of the weapons or warheads at issue and the state which is ahead will not accept the abolition of these weapons unless it considers them peripheral or expects in practice to ignore the ban. Thus, a state's position on the desirability of negotiating an agreement on a particular question will vary over time with changes in the military balance with its potential enemy. When the Soviet Union first tested ICBMs the West proposed that they should be prohibited. When its own weapons were developed it became much less enthusiastic.[33] Conversely, the Russians rejected a cut-off in the production of fissile material for nuclear weapons in the 1960s, no doubt partly because they believed that the US had much larger stocks of such material.[34]

All this may seem both banal and obvious were it not that thousands of hours are spent at New York, Geneva and elsewhere carrying on discussion as though it were only necessary to establish the 'frightfulness' of a particular weapon, or the contribution which its prohibition would make to the halting of the 'arms race', for every right-minded government to agree to its abolition. Moreover the discussion in Western strategic journals on the desirability of a CTBT or a ban on chemical weapons is carried on in much the same way, as though it is only necessary to decide whether these measures are desirable *per se*. Yet agreement can only be reached on these issues by the 'isolationist' approach if in fact they would have no effect on the East-West military balance. This approach provides employment for countless diplomats and UN officials but its contribution to effective arms control is open to question.

It is not only a mistake to isolate individual issues but it is also a mistake to attempt to negotiate major agreements in large and unmanageable fora. Two states may be able to strike a bargain but with every increase in the number of states involved, the problems of reaching a compromise solution greatly increase. The fact is that every state which is not in possession of a particular weapon, which is not thinking of making or purchasing it and which does not rely upon a Great Power ally to use it in its defence, will be in favour of its abolition. This is natural and inherent in the situation since the abolition of such weapons will increase the relative power of the non-possessors and the call for prohibition will improve their image. Certain states, such as Sweden and Mexico, make moralistic attacks on particular weapons into a way of life. But attacks of this sort merely muddy the waters and confuse the issue – and the issue is power. Moreover, they even give states looking for an excuse to increase their forces an explanation for their actions. Thus, France and China explained their decision to develop nuclear weapons by the failure of the existing nuclear weapon states to heed calls at the UN to disarm. It is of course noteworthy that on some really crucial issues, such as SALT, the Great Powers have created negotiating fora excluding states not in possession of the weapons in question. Unfortunately these negotiations are too narrowly focused in terms of the issues under review.

Despite the inadequacy of its provisions for verification and its failure to restrict naval aircraft, the most successful arms control agreement negotiated so far was the Washington Naval Treaty, signed on 6 February 1922. This effectively limited the fleets of the Great Powers for ten years. There are a number of interesting aspects of the Washington Conference. First of all it was extremely wide-ranging, including political and military issues of major importance – the settlement of the Far East and the limitation of navies. Such a conference would certainly be opposed by many today as too ambitious. Secondly, the conference was very short-lived considering the importance of the issues at stake. Secretary of State Hughes sounded out the attitudes of the other Great Powers on the possibility of convening such a meeting on 8 July 1921, the conference met on 11 November 1921, and before the end of the first week in February 1922 the Five Power Naval Treaty and the Nine Power Treaty on China were ready for signature. Agreement was reached at Washington because those involved were prepared to accept some compromises. As a recent historian has written: 'the British and Americans placed in trust with Japan both their trade in Asia and their presence in China and the Philippines. In return, Japan accepted a naval treaty that created a naval balance in the mid Pacific'.[35] That the situation in China was intimately related to the naval balance in the area was nicely demonstrated by the fact that Japan began to prepare to breach the naval agreement at the same time as it began to expand its control over China. Politics and military power cannot be separated into tidy compartments to suit the convenience of diplomats or the tender consciences of humanitarian pressure groups.

One can contrast the success achieved at Washington with the total lack of success achieved at the League of Nations Disarmament Conference. This conference was preceded by a preparatory commission established in 1926. The conference itself met six years later and collapsed in disarray in 1934. Undoubtedly the general diplomatic situation was far worse in 1934 than in 1922 and this made the conference's failure inevitable. But the political atmosphere had not deteriorated between 1922 and 1926 – on the contrary. There were other factors which contributed to the failure of these negotiations: too many states were involved, 25 attended the preparatory committee and about 60 attended the conference itself in 1932; the negotiations were almost exclusively and mechanistically military; and they dragged on for far too long at too low a level.[36]

The British Foreign Office was only too well aware at the time of the futility of isolating military issues in this way. As one official minuted before the conference,

> our aim should be an 'all-in' settlement . . . confidence, which is the only way to recovery, cannot be restored by piecemeal settlements; nor is it likely that one link in the chain e.g. disarmament can be detached for separate examination. It will be necessary to pull the others along with it . . . We ought moreover to welcome the broadening of the basis of discussion, as it makes room for the element of bargaining in which lies our best hope of success, since without give and take on all sides it is almost certain that nothing can be achieved.[37]

The Foreign Office hoped that economic, financial and political issues could be discussed but the conference was already so complicated and so unwieldy that it had to concentrate on technical matters. Looking back, after the conference's failure, the League's own report noted, 'disarmament is only one aspect of an organised peace system and . . . an effort to limit and reduce armaments necessarily entails the discussion of much wider political problems'.[38] But issues of great political, military and economic delicacy could not be discussed in the margins of a great disarmament jamboree. What they required was careful preparation and consideration, followed by confidential discussions at the highest level between the Great Powers.

Too many of the negotiations since 1945 have followed the League, rather than the Washington Treaty pattern. In the absence of a political settlement with the Soviet Union after the Second World War and a formal peace treaty, diplomats turned again to isolating disarmament from its political context, with the same results as in 1932. Some may argue that this was inevitable because of the increased complexity of contemporary issues which makes it vital to discuss them piecemeal. But it is debatable whether limiting nuclear delivery vehicles today is more complicated than limiting battle fleets in 1922. Like the League negotiations, contemporary discussions carry on for far too long. Preparatory talks for the negotiations on Mutual and Balanced Force Reductions (MBFR) in Europe began in November 1972 and the talks were still continuing in 1982. The talks were deliberately made exclusively military and the political questions at issue between East and West were hived off into the Conference on Security and Co-Operation in Europe (CSCE) which also began in November 1972. Undoubtedly the CSCE was too large to negotiate detailed arms control agreements but, as we have seen, there was a sufficient number of political questions involved for agreement to be reached and the Final Act was ready for signature on 1 August 1975.

The essence of this act was the bargain between Western acceptance that the East European borders would not be altered by force and the Eastern acceptance that, in theory at least, they would have to pay more attention to human rights and permit freer movement of people and information between East and West. In contrast, there is no such obvious bargain available so that agreement can be reached in the MBFR negotiations, because they are too narrow and too exclusively military. The West has simply tried to reduce what it considers to be the imbalance between Eastern and Western conventional forces in Central Europe by moral suasion and public pressure. The Soviet Union is offered nothing in return except possibly the knowledge that the armed forces of the Federal Republic of Germany, which it has traditionally suspected and criticised, may be limited by international agreement. Thus, the West has called for reductions of US and Soviet forces in Central Europe by 29,000 and 69,000, respectively.[39] These reductions would be followed by further measures which would create a common ceiling on the central front of 700,000 men. However, not only was it difficult to see what the Soviet Union was supposed to gain from such a proposal but there were interminable disputes about the number of troops already in position.

The wearisome pace and unsatisfactory results of the MBFR talks are in sharp contrast to some of the more successful postwar negotiations, to say nothing of the Washington agreements. The talks on SAL 1 began on 17 November 1969 and the agreement was completed by May 1972. Commentators often blame the asymmetrical nature of the US and Soviet strategic forces for the fact that it took two and a half years to reach agreement. But compromise was possible precisely because of this asymmetry and hence a very approximate balance was attainable between missiles, submarines and bombers. Thus, there were enough important issues at stake to make a bargain possible. If both sides had simply possessed ICBMs, agreement might well have been unattainable.

Where does all this lead to? It seems clear that negotiations on isolated issues of the CCD type can only produce peripheral agreements; that if no bargain is available — as over MBFR — prolonged negotiations will make the situation no better and that isolating the issues at stake from other military questions is the wrong approach. It is also a mistake to attempt to isolate these issues from their political context. The most effective negotiations would combine political and military issues as the Washington conference did. To this suggestion two principal objections will probably be raised — that the arms race is essentially a technical phenomenon unrelated to politics and that no political agreement may be possible.

Military

As we have seen, many commentators argue that the arms race has developed a life of its own independent of East-West relations. Undoubtedly the time which it takes to develop and produce a modern weapon does give the arms race the appearance of being divorced from politics. The Cuba crisis may, for example, have encouraged the Soviet Union to build up its strategic and naval forces. This in turn may have had a major impact almost two decades later. Conversely, one state may attribute the weapons produced by its adversary to current hostility when they are actually the product of events almost a generation old. Furthermore, each state not only has to produce weapons to counter those which its adversary currently possesses but to develop counters to those which it may possess in ten years' time. For all these reasons the relationship between the arms race and the political situation is a complex one.

Nevertheless, armaments cannot be divorced from politics. In periods, such as the 1920s, when international tensions relaxed, so gradually armaments and armies declined.[40] The level of armaments is equivalent to the reading of a patient's temperature. If the political climate, or the patient's condition deteriorates, so the level of armaments rises. The problem is that, unlike the patient's temperature, the rise in the level of armaments may become apparent long after the illness. The fact that Soviet defence efforts did not seem to abate significantly during the period of detente may be due to the continued impetus given by events in the early 1960s, to the absence of public pressure for reductions in the defence budget, to inherent Soviet suspiciousness and unwillingness to place much faith in detente, to the 'threat' from China or to the Kremlin's desire for military dominance. The probability is that all of these factors and many others played a part. The only thing that we can be sure about is that the Russians have as much interest as ourselves in avoiding a nuclear war and it is on this premise that we have to build our arms control agreements and to work towards whatever political rapprochement may be possible.

Some may object that to link politics and arms control explicitly is to threaten strategic bargains which have already been negotiated. Thus, the SAL agreements remain a bargain whether or not the Soviet Union intervened in the Somali-Ethiopian War or invaded Afghanistan. This is true and the appropriate response to these events was not the termination of SALT. However, not only has a strategic bargain to be reached over major arms control issues but it has to be politically acceptable. It is an error, a strategic and political heresy to think that armaments and politics are ever ultimately separable. Critics may also argue that to tie arms control to politics is to restrict what can be achieved. As a result no arms control measures or agreement may be possible. The Western allies frequently linked the reunification of Germany with arms control agreements in the 1950s, implying that one was not possible without the other. A paper produced by the USA, United Kingdom and France in October 1955 argued,

> without German unity, any system of European security would be an illusion. The division of Germany can only perpetuate friction and insecurity as well as grave injustice. France, the United Kingdom and the United States of America are not prepared to enter into a system of European security which, as in the Soviet proposals put forward at Geneva, does not end the division of Germany.[41]

Two years later President Eisenhower agreed with the West German Chancellor, Konrad Adenauer, that a 'comprehensive disarmament agreement . . . presupposes a prior solution of the problem of German reunification.'[42] In the event no agreement could be reached with the Soviet Union on this basis and, when negotiations on European security really began to make progress at the CSCE in the 1970s, they were predicated, as we have seen, on the assumption that Germany would remain divided for the foreseeable future. The NATO countries were right to argue that the reunification of Germany would have settled some of Europe's postwar problems, such as the status of Berlin. In this way it might have led to a reduction of tension. But the Soviet leaders were not prepared to take the risk that a reunified Germany would once more threaten their security. What they rightly saw that they needed was an imbalance between German and Soviet power. Linking military and political questions is not a panacea for the solution of arms control problems, therefore, but without the recognition that there are such links, disarmament and arms control cannot make real progress.

Issues of this magnitude have also ultimately to be handled at the political rather than the diplomatic or military level because only ministers can take the decisions and accept the compromises involved. As a well informed British official wrote of the League of Nations:

> prior to Sir Austen [Chamberlain's period as Foreign Secretary] the government had frequently been represented by Under Secretaries and even by diplomats. These could naturally speak only from Foreign Office briefs and were unable to take responsibility. I have always thought that the manner of the League's death . . . will not be by a dramatic resolution winding it up, but a gradual decay towards inanition caused by States sending diplomats and private individuals to represent them on the Council.[43]

Of course diplomats can shoulder more responsibility today but it is noteworthy that the Partial Test Ban Treaty was negotiated by senior British, US and Soviet ministers in ten days in Moscow in July 1963. Admittedly the speed of the negotiations was partly the result of the peripheral nature of the agreement and the ground had been well prepared by extensive talks on a CTBT. But the danger is that low-level talks may drag on for too long. Speed is sometimes essential because a bargain which one state may make today may become totally unacceptable to it as the political scene and the military balance changes.

Again tight government control of the arms control negotiations will no more ensure success than will linkage with politics. Many of the countries attending the 1932 League Conference were represented by their Prime Ministers or Foreign Secretaries – M. Tardieu, the French Prime Minister represented France, the German Chancellor, Herr Brunning, represented Germany, and so on. But this did not bring success. On the other hand, it is worth noting that the Washington negotiations were largely handled by Secretary of State Hughes himself, whilst A.J. Balfour represented Britain. In recent years British governments have been aware that negotiations at the political level are necessary. Mr Callaghan told the NATO summit conference in Washington in May 1978:

> as soon as there has been some movement in the Eastern position [on MBFR] sufficient to hold out the prospect of real progress we should propose that a session of the negotiations in Vienna should be convened at the level of Foreign Ministers in order to give renewed impetus to the talks.[44]

But, for the reasons discussed above, the moment never came and the talks languished. Negotiating major international agreements on that most delicate of all issues — security — may be likened to opening a combination lock. Not until all the numbers are in the correct order will the lock open. Not until the political, strategic, diplomatic and other conditions are right will agreement be reached.

When East-West relations begin to improve again, as improve they will, the West should try to stabilise and solidify detente by negotiating a wide-ranging politico-military agreement with the Soviet Union. This could combine several of the arms control neasures which have already been well prepared by countless hours of negotiation, including a Comprehensive Test Ban Treaty, further strategic arms reductions and reductions in nuclear and conventional forces in Europe. CBMs could also be strengthened, not only by introducing further notification of troop movements and manoeuvres but perhaps by establishing multinational control posts at key road and rail junctions in Eastern and Western Europe, as was suggested at the abortive surprise attack conference in November 1958. Great efforts would be needed to reach agreement on ways of behaving towards the Third World and, above all, the CSCE measures on human rights and contacts should gradually and methodically be advanced. Such an advance would require adroit diplomacy by Western negotiators but in the long run it could play a part in bridging the East-West divide. If the arms control agreements included in such a wide-ranging rapport were properly verified, the whole package could help to reduce the swings between detente and cold war, which have characterised the post-1945 period and circumscribe ideological competition between the two blocs. In the forseeable future that is the most we can hope for.

Notes

1. 1039 meeting of the UN First Committee, 30 October 1959.
2. For Henry Clay's views see F.W. Wellborn, *Diplomatic History of the United States*, Littlefield, New Jersey, 1962, pp. 72 and 76-8.
3. FO/115/30, Bagot to Castlereagh, 11 March 1817.
4. Loc. cit., Bagot to Castlereagh, 30 June 1817.
5. FO/5/115, Bagot to Castlereagh, 7 August 1816.
6. FO/115/28, Consul General, Anthony Baker to Bagot, 2 June 1817.
7. FO/115/29, Castlereagh to Bagot, 11 February 1817.
8. FO/5/129, Castlereagh to Bagot, 9 June 1818.
9. Loc. cit., Castlereagh to Bagot, 31 August 1818.
10. FO/115/30, Bagot to Castlereagh, 1 September 1817.
11. FO/5/115, Bagot to Castlereagh, 12 August 1816.
12. Loc. cit., Monroe to Bagot, 2 August 1816.
13. See Note 11 supra.
14. FO/115/30, Bagot to Castlereagh, 5 February 1817.
15. FO/5/122, Robert Hall to Bagot, 18 May 1817.
16. FO/414/5.
17. FO/16/356, part 1, Article 1 of the 1881 Treaty.
18. Loc. cit., Minister in Santiago to Salisbury, 12 May 1896.
19. Loc. cit., paper of 7 December 1898.
20. FO/16/356, part 2.
21. FO/16/356, part 1, Minister in Santiago to Salisbury, 16 February 1899.
22. FO/16/356, part 2, Minister in Buenos Aires to Salisbury, 17 October and 26/27 November 1901.
23. FO/16/360, Holdich letter to the Secretary of the Tribunal, 1 May 1902.
24. Loc. cit., Minister in Santiago to the Foreign Office, 17 January 1903.
25. Loc. cit., Minister in Santiago to the Foreign Office, 20 March 1903.
26. Loc. cit., Minister in Santiago to the Foreign Office, 26 May 1903.
27. Loc. cit., Minister in Santiago to the Foreign Office, 19 June 1903.
28. FO/6/490, Minister in Buenos Aires to the Foreign Office, 13 May 1905.
29. The 'humanitarian' case for banning one weapon rather than another is often difficult to make. For example great efforts have been made throughout the twentieth century to control or prohibit chemical weapons. Yet it possible to argue that they were less lethal in the First World War than high explosive.
30. Dusan Pirec, 'Developing Countries and Disarmament', *Socialist Thought and Practice*, January 1976.
31. Sergiu Verona, 'The Geneva Disarmament Committee Some Considerations', *Instant Research on Peace and Violence*, 1-2, 1976. See also M. Fartash, Iranian Ambassador to the CCD, 'The Disarmament Club at Work', *Bulletin of Atomic Scientists*, January 1977.
32. Speech by Mr Callaghan, 2 June 1978, reproduced in UN no. 1, 1978, Cmnd 7267, p. 86.
33. 822 meeting of the UN First Committee, 15 January 1957. See also the Soviet response on 25 January 1957, 828 meeting of the Committee.
34. *Documents on Disarmament 1964*, ACDA, Washington, 1965, p. 339 passim. Soviet spokesmen said, 'we doubt whether attempts to solve this problem outside the framework of General and Complete Disarmament could lead to any useful results'.
35. S.E. Pelz, *Race to Pearl Harbor*, Harvard University Press, 1974, p. 3.
36. A. Eden, *Facing the Dictators*, Cassell, London, 1962, p. 24. Eden said the conference 'was unwieldy, sixty nations sending delegations . . . Committee on committee sprang up and choked themselves with minutely detailed discussions

about the size of aeroplanes or the tonnage of ships'.

37. 'Changing Conditions in British Foreign Policy with Reference to the Disarmament Conference, a Possible Reparations Conference and Contingent Problems', circulated 26 November 1931.

38. Quoted in Major General A.C. Temperley, *The Whispering Gallery of Europe*, Collins, London, 1939, p. 167.

39. L. Weiler and J. Barton, *International Arms Control*, Stanford University Press, 1976, p. 268 passim.

40. M.M. Postan, D. Hay and J.D. Scott, *Design and Development of Weapons*, HMSO, London, 1964, p. 255 passim.

41. *Documents on Disarmament 1945-1959*, Volume 1, p. 530.

42. Loc. cit., Volume 2, p. 788 passim.

43. Temperley, *The Whispering Gallery*, p. 96.

44. Mr Callaghan's speech was reproduced in Cmnd 7267, p. 84.

PRIMARY SOURCES (Public Record Office, London)

Rush-Bagot Agreement
FO/5/113; FO/5/115; FO/5/129; FO/115/28; FO/115/29; FO/115/30; FO/414/5.

St Petersburg Conference, 1868
FO/83/316.

Argentine-Chile Boundary Negotiations
FO/16/356; FO/16/342; FO/16/348; FO/16/360; FO/6/490.

First Hague Peace Conference, 1899
FO/83/1694; FO/83/1695; FO/83/1702; FO/83/1703; FO/83/1704; FO/83/1790.

Second Hague Peace Conference
FO/83/2145; FO/83/2146.

German Breaches of the Treaty of Versailles
ADM/116/2945; AIR/5/398; AIR/5/427.

General Disarmament Negotiations in the 1920s and 1930s
ADM/116/3481; AIR/5/1099; ADM/116/2982.

Chemical Warfare
ADM/116/3618.

Verification Discussions between the World Wars
WO/32/4091; WO/32/4097; ADM/116/3275; AIR/5/1114.

Montreux Convention of 1936
FO/371/20073 consecutively to FO/371/20079.

Postwar
Papers of the First Committee of the United Nations.
Verbatim Record of the Sub-Committee of the UN Disarmament Commission, Cmd 9648 consecutively to 9652.

Further Documents on Disarmament
CMND 1792, 2353, 2595, 3020, 3120, 3346, 3767, 3940, 4141, 4399, 4725, 5011, 5344, 5639, 6512

Documents on Disarmament
Published by the Arms Control and Disarmament Agency, Washington.

ARMS CONTROL AND DISARMAMENT AGREEMENTS

1868 St Petersburg Declaration: Bans the use of exploding bullets.
1899 1st Hague Peace Conference: Bans the use of expanding bullets and projectiles containing poisonous gas, establishes Hague arbitration tribunal.
1907 2nd Hague Peace Conference: Expands the Laws of War to protect non-combatants and prisoners of war.
1922 Washington Conference: Restricts the battleship and aircraft carrier programmes of the Great Powers.
1925 Geneva Protocol: Bans the use of chemical and biological weapons in international wars.
1930 London Naval Conference: Restricts the construction of warships, including cruisers, by the Great Powers.
1935 Anglo-German Naval Agreement: Restricts the size of the German Fleet in proportion to the British.
1936 Montreux Convention: Establishes rules for the passage of vessels through the Dardanelles.
1949 Geneva Convention: Elaborates the Laws of War to protect non-combatants.
1963 Partial Test Ban Treaty: Bans the testing of nuclear weapons except underground.
1963 'Hot Line' Agreement: Improves communications between the USA and USSR for use in a crisis.
1967 Outer Space Treaty: Bans the orbiting of MDW and the use of celestial bodies for military purposes.
1967 Treaty of Tlatelolco: Prevents the acquisition of nuclear weapons by Latin American nations and attacks on such states by the NWS.
1968 Non Proliferation Treaty: Prevents the acquisition of nuclear weapons by more countries.
1971 Seabed Treaty: Bans the emplacement of MDW on the seabed.
1972 Biological Weapons Convention: Bans the production and retention of biological weapons.
1972 SALT 1 and ABM Treaty: Limits the offensive and defensive strategic forces of the USA and USSR.
1975 Final Act of the CSCE: Improves relations between the European states and particularly the NATO and Warsaw Pact nations.

1977 Environmental Modification Convention: Bans the use of environmental modification techniques in warfare.

1977 Geneva Protocol: Increases the protection given to combatants and non-combatants by the Laws of War.

1980 Inhumane Weapons Agreements: Limits the use of incendiaries in populated areas, calls for the marking of minefields and restricts the use of weapons containing non X-ray detectable fragments.

SOVIET AND WESTERN FORCE LEVELS

Any comparison of Western and Soviet force levels is likely to be extremely speculative. Comparisons of defence expenditure are a poor guide to military capability. A developed state, such as Britain, may have a small number of professional but highly expensive soldiers, a Third World country, such as India, may have a large number of inexpensive conscripts. Nevertheless, because such comparisons are made, I have included some SIPRI figures on military expenditure. Comparisons between manpower levels are more straightforward, though even here there are difficulties. Western armed forces may rely to a greater extent than Soviet on civilians for logistic support. Professional soldiers, as in the British and American cases, ought to be better trained than the Soviet conscript. On the other hand, Soviet figures exclude 560,000 border guards, internal security and construction troops which would presumably have some military capability. Finally, reserve forces may play a large part in warfare and yet it is even more difficult to assess their fighting value.

Comparisons between equipment levels should be even more straightforward than manpower comparisons but again there are difficulties. I have used IISS figures for ICBMs and SLBMs but some would say that payload or the numbers of warheads would be a better comparison. Gross figures for numbers of aircraft also hide the difference between a Mig 21 and a Backfire, a Hawk and a B52. I have dealt elsewhere with the problems of estimating foreign military power and I have included these figures only to give some indication why Western commentators and leaders often felt that the Soviet military effort did not decline during the period of detente.

	Numbers in Armed Forces (millions)		
	Soviet	USA	UK
1943/5	19	11.6	5
1948	2.87	1.3	.787
1951	4.6	3.25	.84
1961	3.8	2.57	.45
1971	3.37	2.69	.365
1981/2	3.67	2.049	.343

Numbers of ICBMs

	Soviet	USA	UK
1962	75	294	–
1968	800	1,054	–
1972	1,527	1,054	–
1982	1,398	1,052	–

Numbers of Long-range Bombers

1962	190	600	–
1968	150	545	–
1972	140	390	–
1981/2	150	316	–

Submarine-launched Ballistic Missiles

1962	?	144	–
1968	130	656	16
1972	500	656	64
1981/2	989	576	64

Tanks

1974/5	40,000	10,100	900
1981/2	45,000	11,400	900

Major Surface Combatants

1973/4	212	221	78
1981/2	249	201	62

Attack and Cruise Missile Submarines

1973/4	285	84	28
1981/2	299	84	28

Military Expenditure (Million dollars constant)

1956	31.6	68.2	8.1
1966	47	86.9	8.1
1974	61.1	77.3	9.1

All expenditure figures are from the SIPRI *Yearbook of World Armaments and Disarmament*.

All other figures are from the IISS *Military Balance*, except for the figures for 1943 and 1948.